SALMAN RUSHDIE'S
MIDNIGHT'S CHILDREN

SALMAN RUSHDIE Author and Co-adaptor

Salman Rushdie is the author of eight novels – *Grimus, Midnight's Children, Shame, The Satanic Verses, Haroun and the Sea of Stories, The Moor's Last Sigh, The Ground Beneath Her Feet* and *Fury* – and one collection of short stories, *East, West*. He has also published three works of non-fiction – *The Jaguar Smile, Imaginary Homelands* and, most recently, *Step Across This Line: Collected Non-Fiction 1992–2002*. He is also co-editor of *The Vintage Book of Indian Writing*.

He has received many awards for his writing, including the European Union's Aristeion Prize for Literature and, in 2002, the London International Writers Award. He is a fellow of the Royal Society of Literature and Commandeur de l'Ordre des Arts et des Lettres. In 1993 *Midnight's Children* was adjudged the 'Booker of Bookers', the best novel to have won the Booker Prize in its first 25 years.

SIMON READE Co-adaptor and Dramaturg

Simon Reade is the joint Artistic Director of the Bristol Old Vic Theatre with the director and dramatist David Farr. For Bristol, he has dramatised Jill Tomlinson's *The Owl Who Was Afraid of the Dark*. From 1990 to 1993, Simon was Literary Manager at the Gate Theatre in London with the Artistic Directors Stephen Daldry and Laurence Boswell. In 1997 he joined the RSC as Literary Manager and Dramaturg. During this time he worked in partnership with Tim Supple on *A Servant to Two Masters* and *Love in a Wood* and co-adapted Ted Hughes's *Tales from Ovid*. He also co-wrote and directed *Epitaph for the Official Secrets Act* with Paul Greengrass, and co-abridged Bernard Shaw's *Back to Methuselah* with David Fielding.

After leaving the RSC in 2001, Simon was Head of TV Drama Development at Tiger Aspect Productions and then returned to the BBC as an editorial policy adviser where he had previously worked as a script editor and assistant producer on films by Paul Greengrass, Lee Hall and Stephen Poliakoff, among others.

He has worked as a theatre reviewer and arts journalist for various publications including *Time Out*, *City Limits*, *Financial Times*, *Guardian*, *Observer* and *Spectator*. He wrote the history of the touring theatre company Cheek by Jowl and co-edited, with Alison Reid, the European Classics monologue books.

TIM SUPPLE Co-adaptor and Director

Tim Supple was Artistic Director of the Young Vic from 1993 to 2000 where he directed many successful productions including *Oedipus*, *The Slab Boys Trilogy*, *Grimm Tales*, *The Jungle Book*, *Blood Wedding*, *More Grimm Tales*, *Twelfth Night*, *As I Lay Dying* and *A Servant to Two Masters* (RSC co-production). Productions for the Royal Shakespeare Company include *The Comedy of Errors*, *Love in a Wood*, *Spring Awakening* and *Tales from Ovid* (co-adapted with Simon Reade from the Ted Hughes poems). He has also directed many productions for the Royal National Theatre including an adaptation of Rushdie's *Haroun and the Sea of Stories*, his own versions of *Accidental Death of an Anarchist* and *The Epic of Gilgamesh*, *Romeo and Juliet*, *The Villains' Opera* and *Billy Liar*. Recent productions include *Les Miserables* in Tel Aviv, *Much Ado About Nothing* in Berlin, *Hansel and Gretel* for Opera North and *Tales From Europe* and *Too Clever By Half* at the Norwegian National Theatre in Bergen. He has just completed a film adaptation of *Twelfth Night* to be shown on Channel Four in the new year, and directed an opera version of *Babette's Feast* at the Royal Opera House. In spring 2003, Tim will direct Mozart's *The Magic Flute* for Opera North.

Salman Rushdie's

MIDNIGHT'S CHILDREN

Adapted for the theatre by
Salman Rushdie, Simon Reade and Tim Supple

THE MODERN LIBRARY

NEW YORK

Salman Rushdie's
Midnight's Children

Characters – In Order of Appearance

Mumtaz/Amina
Dr. Narlikar
Nurse Flory
Vanita
Dr. Bose
Mary Pereira
Saleem Sinai
Padma
Dr. Aadam Aziz
Tai the boatman
Ghani the landowner
Naseem/Reverend Mother
Brigadier Dyer
Rani of Cooch Naheen
Mian Abdullah
Nadir Khan
Hanif
Alia
Emerald
Major (Later General) Zulfikar
Adjutant
Lawyer
Priest (A Maulvi)
Newsreel Announcer (Audio)
Ahmed Sinai
Lifafa Das
Midget Queen
Burly Man
Woman
Oily Quiff
Shri Ramram Seth
William Methwold
Homi Catrack
The Ibrahims
Lila Sabarmati
Commander Sabarmati
Wee Willie Winkie
Catholic Priest
Blue Christ
Joe D'Costa
Policemen (Film)

Postman
Shiva
Pia
Nayyar (Film)
House-Manager
Sonny Ibrahim
Jamila
Eyeslice
Hairoil
Glandy Keith Colaco
Fat Perce Fishwala
Zagallo
Masha Miovic
Breach Candy Hospital Doctor
Breach Candy Nurse
Midnight's Children
Parvati-the-Witch
Zia
C-In-C (Later President of Pakistan)
President Iskander Mirza
Ear Nose Throat Nurse
Ear Nose Throat Doctor
Pakistani Army Driver
Ayooba Baloch
Farooq Rashid
Shaheed Dar
CUTIA Soldier
Brigadier Najmuddin
Sheikh Mujib
Four Seductresses
Deshmukh
Indian Commander-in-Chief
Picture Singh
Thin Man
Fat Man
Sari Woman
Little Aadam

Muscular Women, Amritsar Protestors, Protestors Against Partition, Assassins, Wedding Guests, Delhi Street Loafers, Delhi Street Children, Delhi Street Vendors, Language Marchers, Cathedral School Children, Pakistani Top Brass, Hospital Orderlies, Pakistani Soldiers, Professors, Dying and Dead Soldiers, Indian Troops, Magicians, Ghosts.

CAST LIST

This adaptation of *Midnight's Children* was first performed by the Royal Shakespeare Company at the Barbican Theatre, London on 18 January 2003. The original cast was as follows:

Ravi Aujla	**Mian Abdullah/Hanif/Ayooba**
Antony Bunsee	**Tai/Lifafa Das/Deshmukh**
Pushpinder Chani	**Joe D'Costa/Shaheed/Thin Man**
Kammy Darweish	**Narlikar/Ghani/Sabarmati/Fat Perce/C-in-C**
Meneka Das	**Amina**
Neil D'Souza	**Bose/Nadir/Sonny/Zia/Najmuddin**
Mala Ghedia	**Pia/Masha**
Kulvinder Ghir	**Aadam/Picture Singh**
Anjali Jay	**Jamila**
Alexi Kaye Campbell	**Methwold/Zagallo/Priest/Brigadier Dyer**
Shaheen Khan	**Naseem/Lila**
Ranjit Krishnamma	**Homi Catrack/Glandy Keith/Farooq**
Syreeta Kumar	**Alia/Parvati**
Selva Rasalingam	**Shiva**
Tania Rodrigues	**Emerald**
Sirine Saba	**Mary Pereira/Rani of Cooch Naheen**
Kish Sharma	**Zulfikar/Wee Willie Winkie/Mujib**
Zubin Varla	**Saleem**
Antony Zaki	**Ahmed/Fat Man**
Sameena Zehra	**Padma**
Director	Tim Supple
Designer and Choreographer	Melly Still
Dramaturg	Simon Reade
Lighting Designer	Bruno Poet
Sound and Video Designer	John Leonard
Video Designer	Jon Driscoll
Assistant Director	Aileen Gonsalves
Production Manager	Ted Irwin
Costume Supervisor	Jodie Fried
Company Manager	Nick Chesterfield
Company voice work	Andrew Wade and Lyn Darnley
Stage Manager	Jondon
Deputy Stage Manager	Heidi Lennard
Assistant Stage Manager	Simon Sinfield

The production was originally sponsored by Atos Origin

The production was presented in association with Columbia University and the University Musical Society and the University of Michigan, Ann Arbor, USA.

Salman Rushdie's novel *Midnight's Children* was first published in 1981. His five-episode, 290-minute television dramatisation was published in 1999 – after its BBC production was abandoned. This is the first time *Midnight's Children* has been adapted for the theatre. It draws upon the television version as well as the novel.

Its teeming multitudes will be played by an ensemble of twenty. Through-casting, therefore, will be nice and significant, e.g. the performer playing **Tai** the Charon-boatman will also play **Lifafa Das** the peep-show man and **Deshmukh** the scavenger on the battlefields of Bangladesh. The Midnight's Children – on screen and on stage – will be represented by the ensemble.

Midnight's Children tells three main tales: the turbulent history of twentieth-century India, Pakistan and Bangladesh; the saga of a Muslim family; and the story of one man, Saleem Sinai.

Stage directions and original film/sourced footage and music/ sound cues are in italics.

PART ONE

A film screen dominates the stage and shows us the infinite crowd that is India today – a present-day, carnivalesque Independence Day celebration which bleeds into other aspects of modern India, the potent contrasts and diversity of religious and secular, urban and rural, north and south. This montage is accompanied by music.

Tick, tock . . .

We then start to hear **Jawaharlal Nehru** *begin his 'Tryst With Destiny' speech, while the noise of the crowds grows, as Independence looms at midnight, 14/15 August 1947.*

Simultaneously on stage we see two birth scenes in the Narlikar Nursing Home – a nice white linen-made bed with plenty of towels, alongside a basic metal bed.

Nehru Long years ago we made a tryst with destiny. And now the time comes when we shall redeem our pledge. Not wholly or in full measure, but very substantially. At the stroke of the midnight hour, when the world sleeps, India will awake to life and freedom.

In the nice white bed **Amina Sinai** *is in labour, attended by* **Doctor Narlikar** *and the midwife* **Flory.**

Amina Aaa! . . . Aaaah!

Narlikar Yes, push, Amina! Harder! I can see the head!

Amina Just one head, na?

In the plain metal bed, attended by **Doctor Bose** *and the midwife* **Mary Pereira,** *Vanita screams – and dies, as her baby is born.*

Vanita Aahhh . . .

Amina *gives birth at precisely the same moment.*

Amina Aaaaahhhh!

Conch shells blare.

Nehru A moment comes, which comes but rarely in history, when we step from the old to the new . . . when an age ends, and when the soul of a nation, long suppressed, finds utterance . . . we have to build the noble mansion of free India, where all her children may dwell . . .

Fireworks – more conches and the din of independence, the yells, cries, bellows, and the howls of two children newly arrived in the world – out of which . . .

Saleem I was born in the city of Bombay . . . once upon a time.

No, that won't do, there's no getting away from the date: I was born in Doctor Narlikar's Nursing Home on August the fifteenth, *1947*. And the time? The time matters, too. Well then: at night . . . On the stroke of midnight, as a matter of fact. Clock-hands joined palms in respectful greeting as I came . . .

Oh, spell it out, spell it out: at the precise instant of India's arrival at independence, I tumbled forth into the world. I, Saleem Sinai, later variously called Snotnose, Stainface, Baldy and even Piece-of-the-Moon, had become mysteriously handcuffed to history – and I couldn't even wipe my own nose at the time.

He is in a small, disordered office in a dingy building.

Time is running out. I will soon be thirty-one years old – perhaps, if my crumbling, overused body permits. I must work fast, faster than Scheherazade, if I am to end up meaning – yes, meaning – something before I die.

Outside the office, a green-and-saffron neon sign depicts the

goddess Mumbadevi and the words 'Braganza Pickles'.
Inside **Saleem** *sits with a stack of red exercise books, some*
'Braganza Pickles' jars. A strong young woman, **Padma,** *is*
present.

Padma   Eat, na. Food is spoiling. At least try some green
chutney. Your favourite.

She offers him some on a spoon, which he refuses.

Eat up, or Mrs Braganza will be fed up. With me!

Saleem   Food? Padma, I've consumed multitudes. All my
life, I've been guzzling stories. Too many of them.

Padma (*a little confused*)   Eaten too much, baba? Stomach
feels too full?

Saleem   Please believe that I am falling apart – I am not
speaking metaphorically. In short, I am literally disintegrating.

Saleem *pushes aside the exercise book in which he's been
writing.* **Padma** *picks it up and riffles through it.*

Padma   What's with all this writing-shiting?

Saleem   It's my life story.

Padma   You must tell it to me.

Saleem *is pleased, gives a little grin.*

Saleem   I'm warning you: I have been a swallower of lives;
and to know me, just the one of me, you'll have to swallow
the lot as well.

Padma (*settling down*)   Never mind all this swallowing and
guzzling now. What happens next?

Saleem   First I've got to go back to the beginning.

Padma   You already told the beginning. You got born.
'Clock-hands joined palms.'

She puts her hands together, making the pranam.

Saleem   No, no. The beginning of everything, Padma.

Padma   Everything?

Saleem   The time of the holey sheet.

Padma   Holy sheet? What sacrilege is this?

Saleem   I mean, a sheet with a hole.

Saleem *takes a sheet of paper, folds it, tears a semicircle out of the centre, unfolds it: a sheet with a circular hole. He looks through it at* **Padma**.

Saleem   One Kashmiri morning in the early spring of 1915 –

Padma   1915?!

Film: the Dal Lake in Kashmir in its stunning early-morning serenity.

Music.

Saleem   1915 – my grandfather Aadam Aziz hit his nose against a frost-hardened tussock of earth while attempting, somewhat doubtfully, to pray.

Aadam   In the name of God, the Compassionate, the Merciful . . . Ouch!

Saleem   Three drops of blood plopped out of his left nostril, hardened instantly in the brittle air and lay before his eyes on the prayer mat, transformed into rubies.

Aadam *lurches up.*

Aadam   That's it. Finished. Never again will I kiss earth for any god or man.

The old boatman, **Tai**, *approaches, steering his magical boat through the morning mist across the lake's enchanted waters.*

Tai   Ohé! Doctor Sahib!

Aadam   Tai! Is it you?

Tai You must come. Ghani the landowner: his daughter is sick!

Aadam *gets into the boat, clutching his doctor's case.*

Tai So, little Big-Nose. A wet-haired big-nosed child goes Abroad and comes back as a big Doctor Sahib with a bagful of foreign machines. And he's still as silly as an owl. Tell me this, Doctor Sahib. Have you got in that bag made of dead pigs one of those machines that foreign doctors use to smell with? A thing like an elephant's trunk?

Aadam A stethoscope? Naturally.

Tai I knew it. You will use such a machine now, instead of your own nose. A nose like that is a great gift. I say: trust it. That's a nose to start a family on, my princeling. There'd be no mistaking whose brood they were. There are dynasties waiting inside it –

Tai *and* **Aadam** – like snot!

Aadam Agh! Your brain fell out with your teeth, old man!

Tai I am old. I'm so old, that I have watched the mountains being born; I have seen emperors die. I saw that Jesus Christ, when he came to Kashmir – you should've seen him. Christ. Beard down to his balls, bald as an egg on his head. He was old and fagged-out, but what an appetite! I swear he could eat a whole goat in one go. I told him: 'Eat, fill your hole. A man comes to Kashmir to enjoy life, or to end it, or both.'

Aadam *snorts.* **Tai** *taps his left nostril.*

The opulent house of **Ghani,** *the blind, widower landowner. It is dimly lit: shafts of dusty sunlight seep through a fanlight, Vermeer-like, high on one wall.*

Ghani (*to* **Aadam**) A big chance for you, young man. My daughter Naseem is not well. You will treat her excellently. Remember I have friends. Ill health strikes high and low alike. And you have a practice to build.

During which, an enormous white bedsheet is brought on, by **Two Muscular Women**. *There is a hole in the sheet, a crudely cut circle, about seven inches in diameter.*

Aadam   But where is she?

Ghani   You Europe-returned chappies forget certain things. Doctor Sahib, my daughter is a decent girl, it goes without saying. She does not flaunt her body under the *noses* of strange men. You will understand that you cannot be permitted to see her, no, not in any circumstances; accordingly, I have required her to be positioned behind that sheet. She stands there, like a good girl.

Aadam   Tell me how I am to examine her without looking at her?

Ghani   You will kindly specify which portion of my daughter it is necessary to inspect. I will then issue her with my instructions to place the required segment against that hole which you see there.

Aadam   But what does the lady complain of?

Ghani   The poor child! She has a terrible, a too dreadful stomach-ache.

Aadam   In that case, will she please show me her stomach?

A stomach with its tummy button appears in the hole.

Saleem   Far away the Great War moved from crisis to crisis –

Film: First World War, marching soldiers.

– while in the cobwebbed house Doctor Aziz was also engaged in a total war against his sectioned patient's inexhaustible complaints.

In the coming months, Naseem contracted a quite extraordinary number of minor illnesses.

Music.

In the hole in the perforated sheet appear in succession: her right ankle; left calf; right knee.

She waxed anaemic in the summer and bronchial in the winter.

Ghani   Her tubes are most delicate, like little flutes . . . A lump in the right chest. Is it worrying, Doctor? Look. Look well.

There, framed in the hole, is a perfectly formed and lyrically lovely breast.

Aadam (*his voice falters*)   Is it permitted . . . that I touch?

Ghani   Touch, touch away! The hands of the healer, eh?

And touch he does.

Aadam   Forgive me, but is it the lady's time of the month?

Ghani (*nodding affably, slaps* **Saleem** *on the back*)   Yes. Don't be so embarrassed, old chap. You are the family doctor now.

Aadam   Then don't worry. The lumps will go when the time ends.

Saleem   So my grandfather fell under the spell of that magic cloth. He was haunted by the phantasm of this partitioned woman.

And the next time:

Ghani   A pulled muscle in the back of the thigh, Doctor Sahib. Such pain!

And there, in the sheet, hangs a superbly rounded and impossible buttock. A delicious, helpless giggle is heard.

Naseem (*behind the sheet*)   So ticklish, Doctor . . .

Saleem   He was in love.

Music: a lone bugle plays 'The Last Post'. Armistice Day.

And then, in 1918, on the day the other Great War ended, Naseem developed the longed-for headache.

Naseem's face, at last, appears at the hole in the sheet.

Naseem   But Doctor, whatsitsname, what a nose!

Ghani (*frowning*)   Daughter, please. Mind your manners.

Aadam and Naseem are both laughing.

Aadam   Yes, yes, it is a remarkable specimen. A proboscissimus. A cyranose – as my European friends would say. They tell me there are dynasties waiting in it, like . . . (*He stops himself.*)

Naseem   Yes, Doctor Sahib?

Aadam   Like . . . I don't know what.

They all smile and smile and smile.

We refocus on the pickle factory. **Saleem** *looks at the piece of paper with the hole in it.* **Padma,** *with lover-ish attentions of her own, comes up behind him and puts her arms around his neck.*

Padma   So she was beautiful. And they fell in love, and lived happily ever after . . .

Saleem   That isn't how it turned out. He married her. But the trouble's just beginning.

Aadam and Naseem are in bed. He is on top of her. She is motionless.

Aadam   Move . . . move a little.

Naseem   Move where? Move how?

Aadam   Just move . . . I mean, like a woman.

Naseem gives a cry of outrage and pushes him away. She sits up in bed, grabbing the sheet round her.

Naseem   My God, what have I married? I know you Europe-returned men. You find terrible women and then you come home and try and make us girls be like them! Listen, Doctor Sahib, husband or no husband. I am not the moving type.

Aadam   We are going to be a modern couple. You will wear no veil.

Naseem   You will let men look at my face?

Aadam   Men are not beasts.

Naseem   But most men, Doctor Sahib, are also not blind. Walk naked in front of strangers? You, whatsitsname, may be my husband –

Aadam   – That is my last word, wife.

Saleem   How to tell it all? It can't be done.

Padma   Just tell it straight, mister. I'm listening. The whole saga. 'Chapter One' to 'The End'.

Saleem   I can't tell the whole story. I can't tell it whole – it's too cracked. I'm too cracked. Me.

Padma   What?

Saleem   I mean quite simply that I have begun to crack all over like an old jug, that my poor body has started coming apart.

Padma   Back to the story, na.

Saleem   They left Kashmir in 1919.

Slide: black-and-white travel through Raj India.

Padma   Where did they go?

Slide: black-and-white travel through Raj India.

Saleem   Well, they were going to Agra . . .

Slide: Agra.

Naseem *and* **Aadam** *are preparing to travel. Day.*

9

Naseem   Agra University is a famous place, isn't it?

Slide: Agra University.

University doctor's wife. Sounds good.

Aadam   Such a long journey. The train down to Agra after the long road to Amritsar.

Saleem   Amritsar. I can't go on. I'm falling apart. Really.

Padma   The story.

Screen: 'AMRITSAR 1919' in bleak, bold typeface.

Sound: troops load ammunition. This punctuates the scene like a drumbeat – at first indistinct, then crystal clear.

Hotel room: a bed. Night.

Naseem   I do not understand this hartal when nobody is dead. For whom, whatsitsname, this day of mourning? Why will the train not run? How long are we stuck here for?

Aadam   Gandhi has decreed that the whole of India shall come to a halt. To mourn, in peace, the continuing presence of the British.

Sound: a riot is erupting.

Morning.

Naseem   Where are you going?

Aadam   I'm a doctor . . . I have to go.

He grabs his leather bag and is gone.

Naseem (*calling after him*)   You're a madman! That's what you are! Mad!

She subsides miserably on to the bed.

Noises of the rioting mobs. The ammunition loading intensifies. Sound: riot climaxes. Ammunition loading subsides and then builds up again.

Night. **Aadam,** *daubed with Mercurochrome – a red disinfectant – returns to the hotel.*

Naseem (*panicking*)   Let me help, let me help. Allah, what a man I've married, who goes into gullies to fight with goondas! God, you've got blood everywhere! Sit, sit now, let me wash you at least!

Aadam   It isn't blood, wife.

Naseem   You think I can't see for myself with my own eyes?

Aadam   It's Mercurochrome, Naseem. Red medicine.

Naseem   You do it on purpose, to make me look stupid. I am not stupid. I have read several books.

She cleans him up.

Aadam   There is a meeting tomorrow – there will be trouble from the military. They have banned meetings.

Naseem   Why do you have to go?

Aadam   They may need doctors again.

Saleem   History, Padma: history is my fault . . . My poor body. Buffeted by too much history. Coming apart at the seams.

Sound: ammunition loading intensifies, accompanied by armoured vehicles, orders and other military preparation.

The ensemble represents the peaceful protestors assembled in the compound of Jallianwala Bagh.

At the point of the most deadly intensity in the sound, **Aadam** *sneezes.*

Aadam   Yaaaakh-*thoooo*!

Aadam *falls to the ground, as 1,650 machine-gun rounds are fired into the unarmed crowd above* **Aadam***'s head. The ensemble falls. He stands, covered in blood.*

Brigadier Dyer (*the waxed tips of his moustache rigid with importance*)   Good shooting. We have done a jolly good thing.

Naseem   I see you've been spilling the Mercurochrome again, clumsy.

Aadam   It's blood.

Naseem   But *where* have you *been*, my *God*?

Aadam   Nowhere on earth.

Padma   Okay: so never mind Amritsar. What about your mummy and daddy and you?

Saleem   What do you mean, never mind about Amritsar? It started everything! From the Amritsar massacre to Independence night . . . from that dark night to midnight . . . can't you see the connection?

Padma (*sulking*)   It's a crazy way of telling your life story if you can't even get yourself born.

Saleem   Okay, okay: once upon a time this nose, my nose, was on my grandfather's face . . .

Padma   Get to the point.

Saleem   It's 1942 –

Padma   1942? Already?!

Saleem   1942.

A now older **Aadam** *merrily cycles through Agra, whistling an old German tune, 'Tannenbaum'.*

Saleem   That's him. Aadam Aziz. In Agra. In 1942.

Padma   Your grandfather?

Saleem   Yes.

Padma   Looks in a good mood.

Saleem   He was infected with it. Infected with optimism – a

12

highly dangerous strain. It was happening to people all over India that year, and the cause was one man . . . Mian Abdullah.

The **Rani of Cooch Naheen**'s *palace. The* **Rani** *sits on an empire-style sofa.* **Mian Abdullah** *and his secretary* **Nadir Khan** *watch as* **Aadam** *shakes the* **Rani**'s *hand.*

Rani (*introductions*)   This is the famous Mian Abdullah. Doctor Aziz is one of your most ardent supporters, Mian Sahib.

Aadam (*to* **Mian Abdullah**)   You're fighting my fight, sir. Against Partition. Against the Muslim Leaguers.

Rani   Bunch of toadies. Forming governments for the British now that Congress refuses to do it, instead of supporting 'Quit India'. They must be off their heads. Otherwise why this Partition bakvaas?

Mian Abdullah   But we will meet them, face to face. We are fit and ready for the fight. I keep myself pretty fit, Doctor Sahib. Why not hit me in the stomach? Try! I'm in tip-top shape!

Aadam (*smiling, declining to hit his stomach*)   You're expecting a fist fight?

Nadir   Any kind of fight. There is talk of dirty deeds.

Mian Abdullah (*introductions*)   My secretary, Nadir Khan. He has a heightened imagination. A poet, you understand.

Nadir (*embarrassed, shuffles*)   It's true; I have written verses . . .

Mian Abdullah   But what verses! Not one rhyme in page after page! Not even one verb!

Rani   A modernist, then?

Mian Abdullah   Never mind about modernism! Art should uplift, as in our glorious literary heritage.

Nadir   I do not believe in high art. Today art must be beyond the categories. My poor poetry and – oh! – the game of hit-the-spittoon are equals.

Rani   I have a superb silver spittoon, inlaid with lapis lazuli.

She produces the glittering, gleaming spittoon.

Here's a spittoon that's the equal of any poem. Here's a spittoon worth hitting. Let the walls be splashed with our inaccurate expectorating!

They all start spitting – red betel juice – therein, the spitting flamboyant and playful, at first. **Aadam** *leaves. It then develops into the sinister assassination of* **Mian Abdullah,** *behind which:*

Film: stock Hindi movie, black and white. A female cowboy gallops towards the camera. We hear Hindi dialogue with English subtitles.

Gai-Wali (*on screen*)   Yaaaaa! Giaaaa! Eeeeyaaah! Varmints! Doggone bad hats! Non-vegetarians! Free those innocent cows right now! Or I shoot!

Cowboys (*on screen*)   My God . . . it's . . . it's . . . Gai-Wali! Let's run for it!

Galloping hooves. Whinnying horses. Firing of pistols.

Gai-Wali   Run free, cows! Run free, pardners!

Loud mooing of herd of cattle.

Gai-Wali   Run free, cows! Run free, pardners! Thaiii! Thaiii! Blam! Blam! I've got you in my sights, non-veg scum! Hands up, or I shoot!

She shoots. Bang. Bang. Bang.

The home of **Aadam, Naseem** *and their children:* **Hanif, Alia, Emerald** *and* **Mumtaz.**

Naseem   You are cheerful, husband? Good mood? Come

home to fill the kiddies' heads with your nonsense? Foreign languages, whatsitsname, liberal politics and all?

Padma (*horrified*) Who's this? Arré baap, it's your grandmother Naseem? She got old and fat and moley?

Saleem My grandmother, Naseem Aziz, was known to one and all as 'Reverend Mother'; and my grandfather's lack of reverence drove her wild. But when it came to food, her power was absolute. Everyone had to eat whatever she dished out, and only what she dished out: my uncle Hanif, eighteen, and his three sisters, my aunts: bookish Alia, twenty-one; the beautiful Emerald, fourteen; and the dark Mumtaz, nineteen.

Padma (*referring to* **Naseem/Reverend Mother**) It's too bad. That beautiful girl.

Saleem Shhh now. Listen to the story.

Reverend Mother If God meant people to speak many tongues, why did he put only one in our heads? But my maulvi, whatsitsname, who I brought to teach them their own religion? Him, you threw out of the house!

Aadam You know my rule, wife: in this house there will be no veil and no priest.

Reverend Mother What about the rule of Almighty God?

Aadam Your maulvi was teaching them to hate Hindus and Sikhs and other vegetarians. Will you have hateful children?

Reverend Mother Will you have godless ones? Would you marry your daughters to Germans?

Aadam (*changing the subject*) Have you seen the posters? Mian Abdullah is having a rally!

Reverend Mother You can have your Mian Abdullah. But I, whatsitsname, I have the Call of God.

Aadam *rises.*

Reverend Mother   Off again, husband? What a busy life!

He is going to the loo.

Aadam *sits on the 'thunderbox' toilet. In the corner, the washing-chest appears to speak.*

Washing-Chest (*apparently*)   Help me. Doctor Aziz. Help me. Please.

Aadam   What . . . ?

The surprise of the voice has a laxative effect on **Aadam**.

Nadir (*hidden inside the washing-chest*)   I saw it all, Doctor Sahib. I saw everything.

Aadam (*misunderstanding, and gathering his garments around him*)   All? Everything?

Nadir (*hidden*)   The guns. The assassination.

Aadam   What . . .?

Nadir (*hidden*)   Mian Abdullah is dead. I saw it all. Blam! Blam! He didn't stand a chance.

Aadam (*rises from the thunderbox, horrified*)   Who did this?

Nadir (*miserably, still hidden*)   He had plenty of enemies. The British attitude to him was. . . ambiguous. And the Muslim League didn't like him either. He took chances also. Always carried a peacock-feather fan. I told him it was bad luck. He said I should calm myself. Last night he looked at the new moon through glass. Again I told him. . . Bad luck! My 'heightened imagination', he called it. 'Not heightened but frightened,' I said. He laughed. Then they came and surrounded us. There was gunplay and he stopped laughing. How can I calm myself now? That good man is defunct.

Aadam (*opens the washing-chest*)   Nadir. Nadir Khan.

Nadir (*still hidden*)   Pardon the intrusion.

Aadam   Come out of there.

Nadir (*rises*) I must hide, you see. I, through good luck, owing to not carrying peacock-feather fans, owing to not looking at the new moon through glass, survived. But I was his secretary. You have to hide me now.

After a beat, **Aadam** *puts the lid back on the washing-chest to hide* **Nadir**.

Reverend Mother *and* **Aadam** *quarrel as their four children look on.*

Reverend Mother This killing has hurt your brain, husband. How can we keep this strange man in this house full of young unmarried girls?

Aadam He is staying.

Reverend Mother Is this how you show your daughters respect?

Aadam Be silent, woman! The man needs our shelter; he will stay.

Reverend Mother Very well. You ask me, whatsitsname, for silence. So not one word, whatsitsname, will pass my lips from now on.

Aadam Oh, damnation, woman, spare us your crazy oaths!

Reverend Mother *exits, silently, with dignity.*

Mumtaz Where will we put him?

Aadam We will sweep him under the carpet. Like all our troubles.

The scene is transformed from above, to below: the cellar where **Nadir** *is now hiding and* **Mumtaz** *has brought a tray of food.*

Nadir You are very good to me. You are very good.

Mumtaz I am not a brainbox like Alia, or a beauty like Emerald.

Nadir But you are. You are.

Mumtaz At any rate, I'm the one who will look after you. Bring you food and all.

Nadir Yes.

Mumtaz And sweep and clean.

Nadir No! I can sweep!

Mumtaz Even your personal . . . your thunderbox . . . somebody has to empty it.

Nadir You'd do that for me?

Mumtaz Nobody must know you are here. Isn't that right?

Nadir That's right.

Mumtaz Well then. There you are.

Major Zulfikar, *who holds a Wanted poster of Nadir Khan, and his* **Adjutant** *are with the family upstairs.*

Zulfikar Terrible business. Fully understand your grief . . . but you knew this fellow, I believe. The secretary.

Aadam *is impassive.* **Reverend Mother**, *about to speak, is stared at by her family – she remembers she has sworn an oath of silence.*

Zulfikar Met him at the Rani of Cooch Naheen's?

Aadam *is impassive.*

Zulfikar Thought you might be able to shed light on his disappearance. No? . . . No. You've seen nothing of him, then?

Aadam *shakes his head.*

Zulfikar Your son has seen nothing of him.

The son shakes his head.

Zulfikar Nor these charming young ladies of yours.

The daughters shake their heads.

Emerald And if we should see him, Major Zulfikar, what are we to do?

Zulfikar Well, Miss Emerald, naturally you should at once inform your father, who will in turn alert me at my office.

Emerald Of course. Thank you so much, Major.

Zulfikar Right. That's the form. Not to disturb you any further. I'll take my leave. (*whispers to his* **Adjutant** *as he exits*) That girl.

Adjutant Yes, sir.

Zulfikar I may be short-sighted, but I'm not blind.

Adjutant No, sir.

Zulfikar That is the girl I intend to marry.

Adjutant Yes, sir.

They exit.

The cellar.

Nadir You are a brave family.

Mumtaz You are a brave man.

Silence.

Nadir I used to share a room with a painter. A miniaturist. But his pictures started getting too crowded – he tried to get the whole of life into his art. Too much to put in. The canvases got bigger and bigger. They swelled up, you know? As if they were sick.

Mumtaz What happened?

Nadir He killed himself.

Mumtaz My God, killed? (*satirically*) What a romantic saga.

Nadir I'm sorry.

Mumtaz Tell me a poem.

Nadir A poem?

Mumtaz One of yours.

Nadir No, no.

Mumtaz Yes, yes. The best poem you ever wrote.

Nadir The best one?

Mumtaz Nothing but the best will do.

Nadir It's got no rhymes, okay? It's free verse.

Mumtaz Does it have a name?

Nadir Yes.

Mumtaz Then? What is it?

Nadir Mumtaz.

They kiss.

Padma (*excited*) Is this true? There was hankying and pankying? In the cellar? Without even chaperones? With that fat poet? And then?

Saleem And meanwhile, in the world upstairs . . .

Padma No! Never mind meanwhile!

Saleem (*inexorably*) And meanwhile, Major Zulfikar came romancing my aunt Emerald. And Aunt Alia, too, had a suitor: a divorced businessman, a wheeler-dealer from Delhi . . .

Padma (*shrugging*) Who cares?

Saleem . . . and his name was Ahmed Sinai.

Padma (*suddenly interested*) Sinai? But that's your name! Sinai. Saleem Sinai. So Ahmed is your father. So which one was your mother?

Saleem (*teasing*) Amina.

A low-key wedding about to take place: **Aadam** *and his family await the arrival of bride and bridegroom.*

Padma But none of these ladies is called Amina!

Saleem Once upon a time that wasn't her name.

Mumtaz *and* **Nadir** *emerge dressed in wedding garb – she is veiled. They take their places on their wedding chairs.*

Padma She married him? That fat cowardly plumpie in the dark?

The **Rani of Cooch Naheen** *enters accompanied by a* **Lawyer** *and a* **Priest** *(a maulvi).*

Rani Me: *voilà.* As you can all see I'm in perfectly disgusting health. I promised you a lawyer and a priest. Here they are, both utterly discreet.

Aadam A priest, in this house!

Rani Don't sulk, Aadam. This is not your day. Ah, the happy couple. I have a gift for you: the lapis lazuli-encrusted silver spittoon. Poetry and spittoon-hittery, eh, Nadir, my boy? You see, I remembered.

Aadam You must all swear that you will never reveal the presence in our cellar of your new brother-in-law to anyone.

Alia and **Hanif** We swear.

Rani I swear. (She *waves at the* **Lawyer** *and* **Priest**.) And they swear too.

Emerald Why should we swear? What would Major Zulfikar say? You know he thinks Nadir is involved in Mian Abdullah's killing. So if Nadir is innocent he should come out and come clean.

Mumtaz (*enraged*) If he is innocent? *If?*

Nadir Please, Emerald; not yet. There may still be killers waiting. Please, okay. Some more time.

Emerald Okay, okay. Hide on. Hide like a fat earthworm under the ground.

Aadam Emerald!!!!!

Emerald Okay! I swear, for Pete's sake! I swear!

Alia We all swear.

The wedding is performed.

Music.

Saleem Family history, of course, has its proper dietary laws. One is supposed to swallow and digest only the permitted parts of it, the halal portions of the past, drained of their redness, their blood. Unfortunately, this makes the stories less juicy; so I am going to have to ignore family laws.

The cellar has been transformed; it is now a comfortable haven filled with cushions, draperies, lamps, etc. **Mumtaz** *and* **Nadir** *are seated side by side on a large double bed on their wedding night.* **Nadir** *pours her a tumbler of iced nimbu-pani.*

Nadir (*chewing paan*) Oh, Mumtaz. Now you'll have to lead such a strange, double life. A student by day, a wife by night. Buried here in our underground Taj Mahal.

Mumtaz *spits a long, accurate stream of nimbu-pani, and hits the* **Rani**'s *silver spittoon.* **Mumtaz** *laughs with pleasure.* **Nadir** *emits a red jet of betel juice. That, too, hits the spittoon. The newly-weds fall backwards on to the bed.* **Saleem** *sits on the bed while they make love.*

Saleem They called this the Taj Mahal because the famous Emperor's wife was named *Mumtaz* Mahal. And he loved her so much he called her *Taj* Bibi. And when she died, he built a mausoleum for her – the mausoleum immortalised on postcards and chocolate boxes and whose corridors stink of urine and whose walls are covered in graffiti . . .

Mumtaz *and* **Nadir** *break apart, panting, unfulfilled.*

Mumtaz   It doesn't matter, my darling. It doesn't matter, my one and only true love.

Saleem   This underground Taj was their home for two more years, until August 1945. Big month, August 1945. A lot going on.

Newsreel Announcer   Here is the news. A weapon such as the world has never seen has been dropped on the citizens of Hiroshima, Japan . . .

Film: the atomic mushroom cloud – the rumble and boom fade into the thunder of torrential rain.

. . . Here at home, the Rani of Cooch Naheen has died . . .

Ahmed *and* **Alia** *look out into the rain.*

. . . Ahmed Sinai has unfortunately not proposed marriage to Alia Aziz . . .

Emerald *and* **Zulfikar** *hurry through the rain together.*

. . . The situation is growing tense, not least because Major Zulfikar is on the verge of popping the question to Emerald . . .

In the thunder and rain, in the cellar, **Nadir** *vainly attempts to catch the drips in receptacles.* **Mumtaz** *lies in bed.*

. . . A bombshell almost as devastating as Hiroshima is about to explode in the household of Doctor Aziz where Mumtaz is recovering from a mysterious sickness.

Aadam *is at* **Mumtaz**'s *bedside with his old leather doctor's bag.*

Mumtaz   I'm better, truly, Abba.

Aadam (*proud, thinking she's pregnant*)   All the same, I'd better give you a thorough check-up.

Aadam *draws a curtain around the bed.*

Meanwhile **Alia**, **Emerald** *and* **Hanif** *are playing rummy upstairs. Suddenly, the air is filled with a huge roar and they leap up, startled.*

Aadam　Aaaaaaaah!

A thunderclap in the sky.

Aaaaaaaah! Wife, wife!

Aadam *bursts in.* **Reverend Mother** *comes running.* **Mumtaz**, *weak, distressed, comes in in her bedclothes.*

Mumtaz　Please – don't tell them.

Aadam　There has been silence in this house for too long.

Hanif　Abbajan, what is wrong?

Aadam　I'll tell you what's wrong. After two years of marriage . . . my daughter is still a virgin.

Stunned horror from the family.

Mumtaz　I love my husband. The other thing will come right in the end. He is a good man. A marriage should not depend on the thing, but on love. It should not have been mentioned.

Reverend Mother, *towering with anger, erupts – during which* **Emerald** *puts her fingers in her ears and runs from the house.*

Reverend Mother (*three years of silence erupting*)　Whose idea was it? Whose crazy fool scheme, whatsitsname, to let this coward who isn't even a man into the house? To stay here, whatsitsname, as free as a bird, food and shelter for three years? Who was the weakling, whatsitsname, yes, the white-haired weakling who permitted this iniquitous marriage? Who put his daughter into that scoundrel's, whatsitsname, *bed*? Whose head is full of every damn fool incomprehensible thing, whatsitsname, whose brain is so

24

softened by fancy foreign ideas that he could send his child into such an unnatural marriage? Who has spent his life offending God? On whose head is this a judgement? Who has brought disaster down upon this house?

Zulfikar *and* **Emerald** *burst in, followed by the* **Adjutant.**

Emerald (*pointing at the cellar*)   Down there!

Aadam   Emerald, wait!

They all descend. And stop. **Nadir** *is nowhere to be seen.*

Zulfikar   The bird has turned! The worm has flown!

Mumtaz *picks up a note left in the spittoon.*

Mumtaz (*reading*)   'Talaaq! Talaaq! Talaaq!' – I divorce thee, I divorce thee, I divorce thee. That sweet man has set me free.

Saleem   Major Zulfikar didn't charge my grandfather with harbouring a wanted man – but married my grandfather's daughter instead.

Film of a home-movie shot by **Hanif:** *a beautiful wedding – marquees, sweetmeats,* **Guests,** *songs, etc. Ceremony.*

Zulfikar (*to* **Aadam**)   A beautiful wedding, sir. Really most grateful. Damn glad I chose not to charge you. Ha! Ha! Ha!

Ahmed Sinai *deep in conversation with* **Mumtaz. Alia** *observes.*

Mumtaz   I love children.

Ahmed   What a coincidence, so do I . . .

Mumtaz   . . . I didn't have any.

Ahmed   Well, matter of fact, my former wife couldn't . . .

Mumtaz   Oh, no; how sad for you.

Ahmed   Yes, it made her bad tempered, as mad as hell . . . excuse me. Strength of emotions carried me away.

Mumtaz   Quite all right; don't think about it. Did she throw dishes and all?

Ahmed Did she throw? In one month we had to eat out of newspaper!

Mumtaz No, my goodness, what whoppers you tell!

Ahmed Oh, it's no good, you're too clever for me. But she did throw dishes all the same.

Mumtaz You poor, poor man.

Ahmed No – you. Poor, poor you.

Alia (*to* **Mumtaz**) So, gloomy sis, you managed to enjoy yourself after all.

Alia *turns and runs, crying, to* **Aadam**.

Aadam (*to* **Alia**) You're my wise child. You're my brainbox. Too sensible to weep over a man. He's not bright enough for you. No books in his head.

Alia (*snuffling*) But nobody ever married a book. Anyway, who wants to get landed with this marrying business? Not me; never; no.

Padma *is trying to work things out.*

Padma So, Ahmed Sinai didn't marry your aunty Alia. He married . . . Mumtaz, instead?

Saleem Yes. That was the next wedding. Quite soon after.

Padma But then what about Amina? Where's Amina? Isn't it supposed to be her?

Saleem (*laughing*) That's right. Yes it is.

Padma (*much provoked*) Arré, what are you laughing about? You can't even tell a story properly, because goodness knows who's getting married to who-all, and you think *I'm* the one who's funny?

Saleem (*pacifying*) Okay, calm down. I'll just now clear this up.

Train station platform. Hullabaloo. **Aadam, Reverend**

Mother *saying farewells to the newly-weds* **Mumtaz** *and* **Ahmed.**

Aadam (*to* **Mumtaz**) In the end, everyone can do without fathers. (*to* **Ahmed**) The dowry is neither small nor vast as these things go, but we have given you enough. My daughter will give you more.

A green tin trunk, laden with silver samovars, brocade saris, gold coins, is handed over. The train begins to move off taking **Mumtaz** *and* **Ahmed** *away from* **Aadam** *and* **Reverend Mother.**

Ahmed and **Mumtaz** Goodbye! Thank you! Goodbye! Goodbye!

The train picks up speed. Film.

Ahmed I've got something for you.

Mumtaz A present?

Ahmed Better than a present. A new name.

Mumtaz (*puzzled*) Mrs Sinai, you mean?

Ahmed Mrs Amina Sinai. How d'you like that?

Mumtaz/Amina (*doubtfully*) Amina . . .

Ahmed A fresh name for a fresh start. Throw Mumtaz and her Nadir Khan out of the window. Be a new woman in a new life.

Amina (*acquiescing*) Whatever you say.

She snuggles against his arm.

Music and the sound of train.

Padma (*highly excited*) So that's Amina! That's your mother! Arré, good news. I swear, she's the best of the bunch. (*impatient*) So now we're off on a train to Delhi? What about a train to you?

Saleem I'm coming, Padma. I'm on my way.

Delhi. Film/sound: bicycle bells, cacophony.

Lifafa Das *rattling his drum, and wheeling on his peep show.*

Lifafa Das
Come see everything, come see everything, come see!
Come see Delhi, come see India, come see!
Come see, come see!
Come see everything, see the whole world, come see!

Cacophony and film halt midstream.

Saleem I must interrupt myself. It's almost time for a
public announcement. It's January 1947 and I've been
hanging around in the background of my own story for too
long. So, with a sense of high expectation, I look down on
my parents' old Muslim neighbourhood, upon bicycles,
upon street vendors, street loafers, upon little clustered
whirlwinds of flies around the sweetmeat stalls . . .

*We see the hip-jutting, hand-holding, street loafers, the
touting street vendors etc.*

Children rush to see the peep show.

Lifafa Das
Come see come see come see come see!
The whole of India come see!
Taj Mahal in Agra dekho,
Holy Ganges River dekho!
See Mount Everest, come see!
Gateway of India, come see!

Midget Queen Me first! Out of my way . . . Let me see! I
can't see!

Lifafa Das A few minutes, bibi; everyone will have his
turn, her turn; wait only.

Midget Queen I want to see it now.

Lifafa Das *moves another child forward.*

Midget Queen No! No! I want to be first! (*furious*) You've

28

got a *nerve*, coming into this muhalla! I know you: my father knows you: everyone knows you – Badmaash! Hindu! Hindu!!

Boys   Come see Hindu! Hindu! Hindu!

A **Burly Man** *looks out from his window.*

Burly Man   Arré badmaash. Making trouble with my daughter. Raper from nowhere.

A larger crowd gathers.

Woman   Rapist. Arré, my God, they found the badmaash! There he *is*!

Boys   Ra-pist! Ra-pist! Ray-ray-ray-*pist*!

Crowd   Hindu! Rapist! Hindu! Rapist!

Lifafa Das *drags his peep-show box on wheels backwards, pursued by the crowd. He backs into a doorway.*

The door opens, **Lifafa Das** *falls backwards, and* **Amina** *steps forward.*

Amina   What heroes! Heroes, I swear, absolutely! Only fifty of you against this terrible monster of a fellow! Allah, you make my eyes shine with pride.

Oily Quiff   Why speak for this goonda, Begum Sahiba? This is not right acting.

Amina   Go, get out, none of you have anything to do? In a Muslim muhalla you would tear a man to pieces? Go, remove yourselves.

The crowd surges forward.

Oily Quiff   Hand him over. Give him to us.

Amina   Listen, listen well. I am with child. I am a mother who will have a child, and I am giving this man my shelter. Come on now, if you want to kill, kill a mother also and show the world what men you are!

Padma (*clapping her hands in delight*)   You! It is you your mummyji is carrying!

Saleem   That is how it came about that my arrival was announced to the assembled masses before my father had even heard about it.

The crowd disperses.

Lifafa Das   Begum Sahiba, you are a great lady. If you allow, I bless your house; also your unborn child. But also – please permit – I will do one thing more for you.

Amina   Thank you, but you must do nothing at all.

Lifafa Das   My cousin, Shri Ramram Seth, is a great seer, Begum Sahiba. Palmist, astrologer, fortune-teller. You will please come to him, and he will reveal to you the future of your son.

He takes her by the hand and the illogical wonderment of her brand-new motherhood leaders her on.

Music.

Saleem   When you have city eyes you cannot see the invisible people: the men with elephantiasis of the testicles and the beggars in boxcars – and the concrete sections of future drainpipes don't look like dormitories.
When she went to see Shri Ramram Seth My mother lost her city eyes.
Look, my God, those beautiful children have black teeth! Would you believe . . . girl children baring their nipples! How terrible, truly!
And, Allah-tobah, heaven forfend, sweeper women with – no! – how *dreadful*! – collapsed spines, and bunches of twigs, and no caste marks; untouchables, sweet Allah! . . . and cripples everywhere.

Amina   I am frightened, Lifafa Das. Arré baap, where are you bringing me?

They go through a small door: **Shri Ramram Seth** *is sitting*

cross-legged, six inches above the ground. **Amina** *screams.*
Then stops.

Amina Cheap trick. What am I doing here in this
godforsaken place waiting to be told who knows what
foolishness by a guru who levitates by sitting on a shelf?

Lifafa Das O such a too fine fortune he will tell, Sahiba!
Come, cousinji, lady is waiting!

Amina *holds out her palm for* **Ramram Seth.**

Lifafa Das What a reading you are coming to get, Sahiba!
Tell, cousinji, tell!

Ramram Seth *puts his hand on* **Amina***'s womb.*

Ramram Seth A son. A son . . . such a son!

He begins to circle around **Amina** *– we see on screen, briefly,*
the moments he prophesises.

A son, Sahiba, who will never be older than his motherland
– neither older nor younger.
There will be two heads – but you shall see only one – there
will be knees and a nose, a nose and knees.
Newspaper praises him, two mothers raise him!
Washing will hide him – voices will guide him!
Friends mutilate him – blood will betray him!
Spittoons will brain him – doctors will drain him – jungle
will claim him – wizards reclaim him!

Amina What does he mean? I don't understand – Lifafa
Das –

He whirls to a climax.

Ramram Seth He will have sons without having sons!
He will be old before he is old!
And he will die . . . before he is dead!

Ramram Seth *falls suddenly to the floor, frothing at the*
mouth.

Lifafa Das   Begum Sahiba, you must leave, please: our cousinji has become sick. Too much prophecy, man. Our Ramram made too much damn prophecy tonight.

Padma   What did he mean?

Saleem   Shh . . .

Ahmed's house. The bedroom. **Ahmed** *asleep, snores.* **Amina** *watches him, addresses his sleeping form:*

Amina   So, husband. I have learned to love many parts of you – a little at a time:
your over-loud voice;
your vulture-hooded eyes;
(your shortness, which forbids me to wear high heels);
your appetite for fried foods.
I will learn to love the furrow of anger between your eyebrows . . .
But this part . . . even though it is in full working order . . . this, it seems, I cannot learn to love.

Ahmed's *eyes pop wide open.*

Ahmed   Amina?

She is terrified. Has he heard?

Amina   Oh! Did I wake you?

Ahmed *rolls on top of her and they start to make love.*

Saleem   . . . I'm going to have to be quick. Because, unfortunately, he won't take very long. My father had made a lot of money in the leathercloth business, but in those days Muslims with successful businesses were being threatened by Hindu fanatics.

Amina   Not – not so fast – janum! My life . . . !

Ahmed *grits his teeth.*

Saleem   Not only their lives but also their assets were endangered. Trouble was coming. It was only a matter of time.

Amina   Yes . . . so good . . . but a little longer . . . please . . . please . . .

Saleem   He couldn't wait. It had to be right now.

Ahmed (*it is right now*)   Ah, ah, aah!

He subsides. Rolls off her.

We must leave.

Amina   What?

Ahmed   Make a fresh start.

Amina   Where?

Ahmed   Bombay. My friend Doctor Narlikar says property is dirt cheap. The British are leaving in droves. We sell up here; we buy there; the market recovers; we spend the rest of our lives in luxury.

Amina   You – always you decide. What about me? Suppose I don't want . . . I've only now got this house straight and already . . . and the baby . . .

Ahmed   Baby?

Amina   Our baby.

Ahmed   Bound to happen! I knew it wouldn't take long. Well, in that case, it's even more definitely Bombay. Partition is coming and things will get pretty hot around these parts. There will be less trouble down there. We owe it to him to go. That's where he'll be born. Bombay!

Saleem   Our Bombay, Padma . . . !

Film: glamorous Bombay. Sweeping popular period music.

Padma (*encouraging him*)   Yes, mister! We made it! What a journey! Let me see: your grandfather meets your grandmother through a holey sheet, they go from Kashmir to Amritsar . . .

And as she recounts the story we see projected a map of

India with a red line worming its way across the map, following the journey, superimposed over Bombay film.

. . . he almost gets killed, she can't stand being modern, so they fight, they settle in Agra, she gets fat, they have four kiddies, so something must've been working, your mother marries the plumpie who hid in the cellar, but with him something definitely is not working, so out he goes, and in comes your daddyji, and he changes her name, and they go to Delhi, and she saves the peep-show man, and gets a prophecy, and your mummy and daddy jump on the mail train to Bombay, and hey presto! Here they are!

This amazing performance restores **Saleem***'s spirits a good deal.*

Saleem   Wow, Padma, I swear. You know how to tell things really fast.

Film: dissolve to newsreel. **Mountbatten.** *A press conference in the Viceroy's Lodge, Delhi. Flashbulbs.* **Mountbatten** *unveils his 'countdown calendar':* 70 DAYS TO GO TO THE TRANSFER OF POWER, *along with:*

Newsreel Announcer   June 1947! Lord Mountbatten, the last viceroy, begins the countdown to Independence!

Earl Mountbatten   . . . and so I announce the Partition of India. In seventy days' time, we shall leave behind this jewel in our crown, this pearl of the orient, and transfer power . . .

Tick, tock.

Saleem   We are entering my kingdom now, coming into the heart of my childhood. A little lump has appeared in my throat –

June the nineteenth, fifty-six days to go before the British depart. Two weeks after their arrival, my parents entered into a curious bargain with one such departing Englishman: William Methwold.

Methwold*'s house, Methwold's Estate.*

Methwold   I'll sell at this ridiculously low price on two conditions: that you buy the house complete with every last thing in it; and that the actual transfer doesn't take place until the stroke of midnight on Independence Night.

Amina   Everything? I can't even throw away a spoon? Allah, that lampshade . . . I can't get rid of one *comb*?

Methwold   Lock, stock and barrel. Those are my terms. A whim, Mr Sinai . . . my little transfer of power. When India rids itself of us, Methwold's Estate will rid itself of Methwold . . . you'll permit a departing colonial his little game?

Ahmed (*to* **Amina**)   Listen now, listen, Amina. It's a fantastic price; fantastic, absolutely. And what can he do after he's transferred the deeds? Then you can throw out any lampshade you like. It's less than two months –

Methwold (*interrupting*)   You'll take a cocktail in the garden? Six o'clock every evening. Cocktail hour. Never varied in twenty years.

Music: playful.

Film: view from Bombay across the Arabian Sea.

Saleem *introduces us to the following:*

Saleem   Nice people were buying the houses – houses named by William Methwold after the palaces of Europe: Mr Homi Catrack, film magnate, in *Versailles* Villa. The Ibrahims in *Sans Souci* – Sonny Ibrahim would be my best friend.
Next door, in *Escorial* Villa, lived Lila Sabarmati and her husband Commander Sabarmati, one of the highest flyers in the Navy. They had two sons, who became my friends Eyeslice and Hairoil, until I ruined their lives.
– Oh, and *Buckingham* Villa? That was us.

Ahmed *and* **Methwold** *djinn-djinn their cocktail-hour glasses.*

Ahmed   Done.

Methwold   Then everything's tickety-boo. Or, as you say in Hindustani: Sabkuch *ticktock* hai. Everything's absolutely fine.

Tick, tock.

One neighbour, **Lila Sabarmati,** *shows* **Amina** *the Bombay edition of the* Times of India.

Lila Sabarmati   Look, neighbour Amina: it's a catchy human-interest angle to the forthcoming Independence celebrations.

Excited, **Amina** *thrusts the* Times of India *beneath* **Ahmed's** *nose.*

Amina   Janum, look at this.

Ahmed (*reads*)   'Will you have Midnight's Child? One-hundred-rupee prize for baby born at moment of Independence.'

Amina   That's going to be me.

Ahmed   Think of the odds against it, Amina –

Amina   But me no buts. I just know. Don't ask me how.

She feels something inside her womb, gasps.

Such a good, big kick. You see? He knows, too.

Throughout **Wee Willie Winkie** *has been approaching, a talldarkhandsome music-hall clown with an accordion, accompanied by his pregnant wife* **Vanita** *who holds a collecting tin.*

Wee Willie Winkie (*singing – to the tune of 'Nice One, Cyril!'*)
Good night, Ladies! Good night, Ladies!
Good night, Ladies!
We're going to leave you now.
Merrily we stroll along, stroll along, stroll along,
Merrily we stroll along,
For all the world to see . . .

Tick, tock.

Saleem Twenty-five days to go. Twenty-four, twenty-three, twenty-two . . . getting closer!

Methwold (*to* **Vanita**) Sings well, that Wee Willie Winkie of yours. Damn silly name, though.

Vanita You gave it to him.

Methwold *puts a generous contribution in the tin.*

Methwold So I did (*drops his voice*) among other things.

He looks at her womb. She colours and moves quickly away. But **Amina** *has taken note.* **Methwold** *notices her noticing and inclines his head, formally.*

Pretty girl. Must be due about the same time as you. Might give you a run for the newspaper's money.

Amina *turns away from him.* **Winkie** *and* **Vanita** *depart:*

Wee Willie Winkie (*singing*)
    Wee Willie Winkie runs through the town,
    Upstairs and downstairs in his nightgown.
    Rapping at the window,
    Crying through the lock,
    'Are the children all in bed?
    For now it's eight o'clock.'

Tick, tock.

Saleem Eighteen days to go. Seventeen. Sixteen.

Padma Enough Methwolds and Winkies! Tick, tock! It must be time!

Saleem I've had too many fathers, Padma. You have to meet them all.

Padma What nonsense you talk. Just get on with it.

Saleem There's one more father you have to meet. Because he was my father, in a way.

Padma Who?

Saleem He was called Joe. Joseph D'Costa. And he had his Mary, too. Mary Pereira, nurse at Doctor Narlikar's Nursing Home. Now at confessional.

St Thomas's Cathedral. The wooden latticed window of the confessional. A blue-faced Christ on a crucifix.

Priest Blue.

Padma The priest? That father?

Saleem No. Not him. Patience, Padma.

Priest All available evidence, my daughter, suggests that Our Lord Christ Jesus was the most beauteous, crystal shade of pale sky blue.

Mary But how, Father? People are not *blue*. No people are blue in the whole big world!

Priest God is love; and the Hindu love-god, Krishna, is always depicted with blue skin. Besides, blue is a neutral sort of colour, neither black nor white . . .

Mary What type of answer is blue, Father, how to believe such a thing? You should write to Holy Father Pope in Rome, he will surely put you straight; but one does not have to be Pope to know that the mens are not ever blue!

Priest Skins have been dyed blue. The Picts; the blue Arab nomads; with the benefits of education, my daughter, you would see –

Mary What, Father? You are comparing Our Lord to *junglee* wild men? O Lord, I must catch my ears for shame!

Priest Come, come, surely the Divine Radiance of Our Lord is not a matter of mere pigment?

Mary Which is what I told him.

Priest Him?

Mary   Joe. Joseph

Priest (*pleased with himself*)   You, a Mary, have your Joseph.

Mary   Joseph D'Costa. He's an orderly where I'm a nurse, at Doctor Narlikar's Nursing Home. Suddenly suddenly he's sniffing the air all the time – (to **Joe**) you got a cold or what, Joe?

Joe *has entered in parallel time.*

Joe   No. I'm sniffing the wind from the north.

Mary   But Joe, in Bombay the wind comes off the sea, from the west, Joe . . .

Joe   You don't know nothing, Mary, the air comes from the north now, and it's full of dying. This Independence is for the rich only; the poor are being made to kill each other like flies. In Punjab, in Bengal. Riots riots, poor against poor. It's in the wind.

Mary   You talking crazy, Joe, why you worrying with those so-bad things? We can live quietly still, no?

Joe   Never mind, you don't know one thing.

Mary   But Joseph, even if it's true about the killing, they're Hindu and Muslim people only; why get good Christian folk mixed up in their fight? Those ones have killed each other for ever and ever.

Joe   You and your Christ. You can't get it into your head that that's the white people's religion? Leave white gods for white men. Just now our own people are dying. We got to fight back; show the people who to fight instead of each other, you see?

Mary (*to* **Priest**)   White gods. That's why I asked about colour, Father.

Tick, tock.

Saleem Two days to go . . . one . . . and we're there. It's tonight.

Saleem *gets up from his desk and heads for the door.*

Padma Hey! Where do you think you're going? You can't just buzz off if it's time.

Saleem I'm going to have a bath, and shave, and put on clean clothes. I'm going to brush my hair and clean my teeth. I'm about to be born. I intend to look my best.

Tick, tock.

Amina Arré Ahmed! Janum, the baby! It's coming – bang on time!

Tick, tock! Tick, tock!

Film: we see, again, flashes of the prophecies . . . Simultaneously, we see two birth scenes in the Narlikar Nursing Home – a nice white linen-made bed with plenty of towels, alongside a basic metal bed. In the nice white bed **Amina Sinai** *is in labour, attended by* **Doctor Narlikar** *and the midwife* **Flory**. *In the plain metal bed, attended by* **Doctor Bose** *and the midwife* **Mary Pereira**, **Vanita** *wrestles with labour.* **Ahmed** *and* **Wee Willie Winkie** *prowl the corridor outside.*

Tick, tock!!!! Tick, tock!!!!

On his Estate, **Methwold** *raises a glass, downs a whisky, saluting a sinking Union flag.*

Wailing and shrieking from **Amina** *and* **Vanita** *– in the streets it's as if a monster has begun to roar.*

Amina*'s bed.*

Amina Aaa! . . . Aaaah!

Nehru*'s speech runs throughout the births.*

Nehru A moment comes, which comes but rarely in history, when we step from the old to the new . . .

Narlikar   Yes, push, Amina! Harder! I can see the head!

Amina   Just one head, na?

Nehru   . . . when an age ends, and when the soul of a nation, long-suppressed, finds utterance . . .

Vanita's *bed: she screams – and dies as her baby is born.*

Vanita   Aahhh . . .

Amina *gives birth at precisely the same moment.*

Amina   Aaaaahhhh!

Nehru   . . . we have to build the noble mansion of free India, where all her children may dwell . . .

Conch shells blare – the howls of two children newly arrived in the world – the din of Independence – fireworks, saffron and green.

Flory *takes* **Amina**'*s baby to the front of the stage to lay it, kicking and screaming, into a crib – and then returns to* **Amina**.

Doctor Bose *covers* **Vanita**'*s bloody corpse.* **Mary Pereira** *holds the late* **Vanita**'*s squalling baby.*

Doctor Bose   Nothing more we can do here.

Mary *moves to the front of the stage to place* **Vanita**'*s baby in its crib alongside* **Amina**'*s baby. She is about to attach a tag to its ankle – when* **Joe D'Costa** *appears behind her and puts his hand over her mouth.*

Joe   It's okay. It's me. Mary, it's me.

She turns to him with a mixture of relief and fear – and sees his filthy state.

Mary   Joe! Where've you been?

Joe   They're after me. I need money for the train.

She takes out her purse – he takes all the money she's got.

Mary   Joe, I told you and told you . . .

He's already looking to leave.

Joe   We have to do it now, Mary. The real revolution. The rich must fall; then we'll have our freedom.

He goes to the open window and without a word of farewell, ducks outside on to the fire escape – and is gone. We follow him on screen.

Mary (*softly to the departed* **Joe**)   Say you love me, Joe. Say it once before you go.

She stops. Looks at **Amina**'s *baby and its tag. Back at* **Vanita**'s *baby and its tag. Baby to baby. Tag to tag.*

Mary   Joseph. I'm doing this for you, Joseph. Let the poor be rich, and the rich, poor.

She switches the tags.

Saleem   And it was done.

Film: **Joe D'Costa** *is hotly pursued by* **Police**.

Policeman   Halt! Or we'll fire . . .

Film: **Joe** *keeps running. The* **Police** *shoot him dead.*

Mary *walks up to a weeping* **Winkie** *with a tagged and swaddled child.*

Flory *picks up the remaining tagged and swaddled child and gives him to* **Amina** – **Ahmed** *is by her side.*

The tragic figure of **Winkie** *with his swaddled child makes his way through the Independence crowd.*

Padma *is furious with* **Saleem**, *paces the pickle factory.*

Padma   She swapped the babies? That Mary? Poor for rich, rich for poor?

Saleem *spreads his hands, apologetically.*

Padma   You tricked me. Your mother, you said. Your father,

your grandfather, your aunts. What kind of thing are you?
You don't care that your real mother died giving you birth?

Saleem (*quietly*)   I do care.

Padma (*working things out)*   And so, if Vanita . . . and that
baldy Englishman, Methwold . . . (*horrified*) Then you're an
Anglo, isn't it? Half and half!

Saleem (*wretched*)   Even my name is not my own.

Padma *sees his sadness, her anger fades. She embraces him.
Her caresses grow insistent.*

Padma   Shhh. No more stories tonight. Come on. Let's see
if we can make your other pencil work.

Saleem   Padma . . . it's no use . . .

He picks up a framed newspaper clipping and reads.

'Midnight's Child.
A charming pose of Baby Saleem Sinai, who was born last
night at the exact moment of our Nation's independence –
the happy Child of that glorious Hour!'

You know what the prize was? Just one hundred rupees!
Not much historical significance there. Just a cheap stunt.

Padma   Don't be vain. Everybody gets born, after all. It's
not such a big big thing.

Saleem   No, Padma, this is important . . .

Padma (*explodes*)   Important? Why, when you care more
for some old photo than for me?

Saleem   If you love me, you must understand.

Padma   Love you? Love you? What use are you, little
princeling, as a lover?

And out she storms, slamming the door.

Saleem (*morose*)   Not just a photo, Padma. There were
other signs, too. Signs that I was going to *mean* something.

43

That I couldn't escape it. *History*, Padma. Everything that happened, happened because of me . . . India, the new myth, the dream we all shared, a collective fiction. All over the new India children were being born who were only partially the offspring of their parents. The children of midnight were also the children *of the time*, fathered, you understand, by history. I was already beginning to take my place at the centre of the universe and by the time I had finished I would give meaning to it all.

I had arrived.

A **Postman** *arrives at Buckingham Villa, Methwold's Estate.*

Postman   Letter, madam! Look, madam! Government letter!

Amina (*reads the letter*)   'Dear Baby Saleem, Congratulations on the happy accident of your moment of birth! We shall be watching over your life with the closest attention; it will be, in a sense, the mirror of our own. Signed, Jawaharlal Nehru.'

Postman   The government, madam? It will be keeping one eye on the boy? But why, madam? Something is wrong?

Amina (*laughing*)   It's just a way of putting things. It doesn't really mean what it says.

The **Postman** *departs.* **Mary Pereira** *approaches and is guiltily startled to see* **Wee Willie Winkie** *carrying the swathed* **Baby Shiva.**

Winkie (*singing* 'Somewhere over the Rainbow')

He breaks off.

You were at the hospital.

Mary (*panicky*)   Yes.

She throws some coins in his hat – too many coins – and rushes off. He picks up the hat and the money and leaves, looking a little puzzled.

Winkie (*singing* 'Somewhere Over the Rainbow')

And he's gone. **Mary** *is now at the house, on the veranda.*

Mary   Madam . . .

Amina   Hullo. Nurse Mary, isn't it? Has Doctor Narlikar sent you? Is anything the matter?

Mary   No . . . Doctor Narlikar does not know, madam. And the only matter is . . . you see . . . I was thinking, madam . . . Are you maybe by any chance in need of an ayah?

Amina   Why, Mary! You know, I think I am.

They approach **Baby Saleem***'s cot.*

Mary   You see, I have fallen for your beautiful child. First time I saw him I was done for. I love him, madam. Like the child of my own heart.

She takes **Baby Saleem***, and cradles him.*

Madam, look. He is not blinking. Look how he stares at me.

Amina   Mary, you're right.

Mary   Blink! Little one, blink! In this life, no one should keep their eyes open all the time.

Baby Saleem *is now happily blinking.*

Amina   My little Piece-of-the-Moon!

The song of **Mary Pereira**
   Anything you want to be you can be;
   You can be just what-all you want . . .

And as she sings, she puts **Baby Saleem** *to bed.*

Saleem   It was the kind of song that sets history in motion. But it's history that unmanned me – as it unmanned my father before me. . . soon after I was born, the government froze all my father's assets. Catch a lizard by the tail and he'll snap it off to escape. Freeze a Muslim's assets, and he'll run off to Pakistan leaving his wealth behind. That was the idea. So: bank accounts, property rents, everything was frozen. Overnight.

Must have been the baby photo in the paper. Otherwise why pick on us?

Ahmed *is sitting up in bed with a glass of whisky.* **Amina** *trying to comfort/seduce him.*

Ahmed The bastards have shoved my balls in an ice bucket!

Amina We'll fight them, janum. We'll win. Come here now . . . oh, my goodness, it's true! Soooo cooold! Like little round cubes of ice!

Saleem That night my sister Jamila was – quickly – conceived.

. . . Let me tell you something about history. It's like snakes and ladders. While my father slid down a snake into a bottle of whisky, my uncle Hanif's career as a film director was at its peak.

Film: on the screen we are watching The Lovers of Kashmir, **Hanif**'s *film starring his wife, the divine* **Pia.**

A pregnant **Amina** *(***Jamila** *in her womb),* **Ahmed, Hanif** *and* **Pia** *attend its glittering Bombay premiere, their faces lit by the flickering light of the film.*

Saleem My uncle Hanif's first big movie. *The Lovers of Kashmir.* Starring his beautiful wife: my auntie Pia. Produced by Homi Catrack –

Homi Catrack's *hand strays to* **Pia**'s *knee – she strokes it, then moves it away.*

Saleem   – the rotter. And my mother pregnant again, my sister in her womb.

Hanif (*whispering to* **Amina**)   Watch this. I've beaten the censor.

*Film: on the screen, after a few pleasantries, **Pia** and her on-screen lover, **Nayyar**, start to kiss – not one another – but things: **Pia** kisses an apple, sensuously, and passes it to **Nayyar**, who kisses the opposite side of the apple with equal passion.*

In the cinema: there is a low buzz of shock from the audience.

Saleem Padma: if only you were here. 'No kissing on screen,' said the rules for film-makers, 'to avoid corrupting the morals of national youth.' But they had to permit . . . this.

Film: on the screen, this manner of kissing between the two continues on cups of pink tea, on swords, on mangoes . . .

*In the cinema: the house lights go up. Groans of disappointment from the audience. An ineffectual **House Manager** shuffles forward.*

*Film: on the screen, the actors **Pia** and **Nayyar** also stop what they're doing and stare down at the **House Manager**.*

House Manager Ladies and gents. There is terrible news. (*His voice breaks.*) This afternoon, at Birla House in Delhi, our beloved Mahatma was killed. Some madman shot him in the stomach, ladies and gentlemen – our Bapuji is gone!

*Film: on the screen, **Pia** and **Nayyar** react with horror.*

Hanif (*to **Amina***) Get out of here, big sister – if a Muslim did this, there will be hell to pay.

Amina (*to **Ahmed***) Ahmed. . . the baby. It's time.

Ahmed (*thickly – he's been drinking*) Now? What sort of time is this to have a baby?

Saleem Snakes and ladders. Death of the Mahatma: big snake. It turned out the killer wasn't a Muslim: huge relief in our house. Bit of a ladder there, you could say. But here comes a long ladder. Over nine years long. And here at the end of it is my sister Jamila, already eight years old.

We see **Jamila,** *her face daubed with boot polish, wearing a Red Indian headdress, a tomboy to a T. She's carrying shoes.*

And here are my friends, marching home from school.

The Cathedral School **Chums** *– white-shorted, wearing blue-striped elastic belts with S-shaped snake buckles.*

Film: the Language Marchers.

Up there, by the way, history's marching on. This was the time of the Language Marches. The Language Marchers wanted the state of Bombay to be cut into two states, one for Marathi speakers, the other for Gujarati speakers.

As for us? We spoke English.

Sonny   Chiquitas! Toro, toro!

Saleem   Sonny Ibrahim. And Eyeslice:

Eyeslice   Hi, Saleem!

Saleem   And his brother Hairoil:

Hairoil   Hiya!

Saleem   And Glandy Keith Colaco and Fat Perce Fishwala – well, these two weren't really my friends.

Sonny   Chiquitas! Toro, toro! . . . When I grow up, I'm going to be a bullfighter: Chiquitas! Hey, toro, toro!

Sonny *holds his satchel as if he's taunting the bull.*

Glandy Keith   I'm going to run my dad's cinemas. Keith's Talkies! Keith's Empire. You bastards want to watch movies, you'll have to come an' beg me for seats! Except Fat Perce here.

Fat Perce   Bah! That's nothing! I'll have diamonds and emeralds and moonstones! Pearls as big as my balls!

Eyeslice (*he only has one eye*)   I'm going to be a Test Cricketer (*mimes strokes*) And another four! Six!

48

Hairoil Selfish bums! I'm going into the Navy like our father; I shall defend my country!

Hairoil *is pelted with rulers, compasses, inky pellets . . .*

Glandy Keith (*to* **Saleem**)   Hey, Snotnose! Hey, whaddya suppose our Sniffer'll grow up to be?

Fat Perce   Pinocchio!

They all sing the song from the Disney movie: 'I've Got No Strings'.

All   Pinocchio! Cucumber-nose! Goo-face!

Glandy Keith *and* **Fat Perce** *exit. As* **Sonny, Saleem, Eyeslice** *and* **Hairoil** *make their way home, they pass* **Wee Willie Winkie** *singing 'How much is that doggy in the window?'*

A baleful nine-year-old **Shiva** *sits at his feet, glaring at the rich kids.*

Sonny (*to* **Saleem**)   Listen, Saleem, man, don't let that Fat Perce and Glandy Keith get you down. Isn't it, Eyeslice?

Eyeslice   They're just bullies, yaar. You don't look so bad. Hey (*pointing mockingly at* **Shiva**), not as bad as him!

Shiva *leaps up, grabs a handful of stones, and begins throwing them at the alarmed boys. They run.* **Winkie** *grabs* **Shiva**'s *arms.*

Winkie   Stop it! Stop it at once!

Shiva *turns on* **Winkie** *and starts to kick and punch –* **Winkie** *cowers as the blows rain down.* **Saleem** *and his friends stop their flight and watch this in amazement – then they hurry away.*

Young Saleem *arrives home with* **Sonny**.

Ahmed (*whisky in hand, his voice over-emotional*)   Come to me, my boy! Come, my only son!

He embraces **Young Saleem**.

Young Saleem   Stop, Abba! Everyone will see.

Ahmed   Let them look! Let the whole world see how I love my son! No limits for you, my boy! Great things in store! What's that smell?

Jamila *has set fire to the pile of shoes she was carrying earlier.*

Saleem   In the summer of 1956, while the Language Marchers marched, my sister was setting fire to our neighbours' shoes.

Mary Pereira *dashes on to douse the flames.*

Amina   You . . . Jamila. Go to your room! And no talking for one whole day.

Sonny *is staring at* **Jamila** – **Young Saleem** *is miffed/jealous.*

Jamila (*as she exits*)   What are you staring at, Sonny?

Sonny   Um. Um, you . . . Saleem's sister . . .

Jamila   What do you want?

Sonny   I'm, you know . . . damn keen on you.

Jamila *smiles her sweetest smile, comes very close to* **Sonny**, *and knees him in the balls* – **Young Saleem** *is delighted at* **Sonny**'s *discomfort.*

Sonny   Owww . . .

Amina (*to* **Jamila**)   Shoo!

The phone is ringing simultaneously in Buckingham Villa as in the pickle factory.

Pickle factory.

Saleem (*picks up receiver*)   Hullo? Hullo? Padma? Is that you? (*His face falls.*) No, no. No, not a truck company. Sorry. Wrong number.

He replaces the receiver.

Buckingham Villa.

The phone is ringing and is answered by **Amina.**

Amina   Hello?

Young Saleem *and* **Jamila** *eavesdrop.*

Amina   Sorry: wrong number. (*then,* sotto voce) When?
Where? (*then, normal voice*) I told you. Wrong number.

*She replaces the receiver, looking upset. She gets her car keys
and departs.*

Jamila *emerges.*

Young Saleem   Where does she go?

Jamila   Smuggling? No: spying!

Young Saleem   No, yaar . . .

Jamila (*shrugging*)   Who cares? Believe, don't believe. But
it's a mystery, that's the truth.

Saleem   That was not good enough for me – this was only
one of the many mysteries of being alive I could not bear.
So, like Nadir Khan before me, I sought the refuge of pants
and vests and made my hideaway in my parents' washing-
basket.

Young Saleem *enters the bathroom and climbs into the
washing-chest, closing the lid after him.*

Saleem   In those days my nose was permanently blocked.
So I didn't have to worry about the smell.

The bathroom door opens and **Amina** *comes in, back from
her outing. She sits on the closed lid of the thunderbox loo,
weeping. And mumbling.*

Amina   Na. Dir. Na. Dir. Nadir. Nadir.

*She begins to remove her sari, clasp her breasts, hand
straying below her waist, between her thighs.*

Yes, Nadir. We did this, my love. It was enough. Enough for me. Nadir. Oh . . . yes. Yes.

From within the washing-chest, **Young Saleem** *lets out a cataclysmic, world-altering sneeze!*

Young Saleem   AHHH-CHHHOOOO . . . !

And he hits his nose – which starts to bleed.

OWWW!!

Amina *leaps to her feet appalled, hurriedly gathers her sari and opens the washing-chest.*

Amina   Who's there?

Laundry and **Young Saleem** *come tumbling out at her feet.*

Young Saleem   I didn't look, Ammi, I swear!

Then his face changes, he's hearing things, voices in his head, hundreds of people talking at once, incomprehensible – we still hear the **Language Marchers** *who have been gathering earlier – and* **Young Saleem** *yelps.*

Ammi, I hit my nose . . . There's noise . . . !

Amina *grabs him by the ear.*

Amina   Noise? You just come on with me.

She drags him to **Ahmed** *and* **Mary** *and* **Jamila.**

Noise, like the crackling of a badly tuned radio – **Young Saleem**'s *hearing the racket of voices in his head – while outside the* **Language Marchers** *are chanting.*

Marchers
    Sundar Mumbai Marathi Mumbai!
    Sundar Mumbai Marathi Mumbai!
    [Beautiful Bombay Marathi Bombay]
    Maharashtra! Maharashtra! Maharashtra!

Ahmed   So, Saleem. You have something to say for yourself. An apology, I hope.

Young Saleem   I'm hearing voices. Voices are speaking to me inside my head.

Jamila   God, Saleem. All this tamasha for one of your silly cracks!

Mary (*crossing herself*)   Holy Father in Rome.

Amina   Catch your ears for shame! You will bring down the roof upon our heads. What has happened to my darling baby boy – are you mad?

Young Saleem   But, Ammi, it's true.

Ahmed   Noises in your ear? I'll give you noises in your ear.

Ahmed's *hand delivers* **Young Saleem** *a mighty blow to the side of his head.* **Young Saleem** *falls sideways, reeling out of the house and into the path of the* **Marchers**.

Marchers
    Sundar Mumbai Marathi Mumbai!
    Sundar Mumbai Marathi Mumbai!
    [Beautiful Bombay Marathi Bombay]
    Maharashtra! Maharashtra! Maharashtra!

Marchers   Who's this?/A little laad-sahib come down to join us from the big rich hill!/You been in a fight, little princeling?

Young Saleem *shakes his head.*

Marchers   Oho! The young nawab does not like our tongue!/Speak, little master./Speak before we slit your throat and finish the job./You don't like Maharashtra, my little lord?/Are you for Gujarati, then?/Speak, little master!/Speak some Gujarati!

Young Saleem   Please sirs. I only know one stupid Gujarati rhyme.

Marcher   Out with it.

Young Saleem *pauses, then quietly mutters*:

Young Saleem
  Soo ché? Saru ché!
  Danda lé ké maru ché!

Marcher   Means what?

Young Saleem
  How are you? I am well!
  I'll take a stick and thrash you to hell!

The **Marchers** *pause – then laugh.*

Marcher   Too good! I swear!

Then they all take up the chant with relish:

Marchers
  HOW ARE YOU? I AM WELL!
  I'LL TAKE A STICK AND THRASH YOU TO HELL!

And the march turns into a wounding, murderous riot. Film. The sound of the riot merges with the sound of the Midnight's Children.

Saleem   To the tune of my little rhyme, the first language riot took place. Fifteen killed. Two hundred and sixty-six wounded. Thus I triggered the violence that would lead to the partition of the state of Bombay and breed such killings in perpetuity.

But I have another story to unfold.

1958. Morning. At the Cathedral School. Double geography with **Zagallo**. **Glandy Keith Colaco, Fat Perce Fishwala, Eyeslice, Hairoil, Sonny, Young Saleem,** *etc.*

Zagallo (*who has a barbarian's shaggy moustache*)   Okey-dokey, jungle-Indians and bead-lovers: you see heem, you savages? (*pointing at a print of a soldier in pointy tin hat and metal pantaloons*) Thees man eez civilisation! You show heem respect: he's got a *sword*!

He swishes his cane.

Human geography. Thees ees *what*? Sonny Ibrahim?

Sonny   Please sir don't know sir.

Lots of hands go up, but **Zagallo** *buffets* **Sonny**, *and twists him by the ear.*

Zagallo   Feelth from the jungle, stay in class sometimes and find out!

Sonny   Ow ow ow yes sir sorry sir . . .

Young Saleem   Sir please stop sir he has a heart condition sir!

Perce   A heart condition caused by Snotnose's sister, sir . . .

Guffaws from the class.

Zagallo (*to* **Young Saleem**)   So, a leetle arguer, ees eet?

He leads **Young Saleem** *by his hair to the front of the class.*

So answer the question. You know what ees human geography?

Young Saleem (*in pain beneath his gripped tuft of hair*) Aiee sir no sir ouch!

Zagallo *smiles and between thumb and forefinger, pulls* **Young Saleem** *downwards by the nose.*

Zagallo   See, boys – you see what we have here? Regard, please, the heedeous face of thees primitive creature. It reminds you of?

Boys   Sir the devil sir/Please sir one cousin of mine!/No sir a vegetable sir I don't know which.

Zagallo   Silence! Sons of baboons! Thees object here (*he tugs* **Young Saleem**'s *nose*) *thees* is human geography!

Boys   How sir where sir what sir?

Zagallo (*guffawing*)   You don't see? In the face of thees ugly ape you don't see the whole map of *India*?

Pause.

Boys   Yes sir no sir you show us sir!

Zagallo   See here – the Deccan peninsula hanging down!

Young Saleem *in ouchmynose agony.*

Glandy Keith   Sir sir if that's the map of India what are the stains sir?

The **Boys** *snigger, titter.*

Zagallo   These stains are Pakistan! Thees birthmark on the right ear is the East Wing; and thees horrible stained left cheek, the West! Remember, stupid boys: Pakistan ees a stain on the face of India!

Boys   Ho ho, absolute master joke, sir!

Fat Perce   Lookit that, sir! The drip from his nose, sir! Is that supposed to be *Ceylon*?

Young Saleem*'s nose has plopped snot on to* **Zagallo***'s hand.*

Zagallo   Animal, you see what you do?

He releases **Young Saleem***'s nose but grabs him by the hair again.*

What are you? Tell me what you are!

Young Saleem (*forced on to tiptoes*)   Sir an animal sir!

Zagallo (*pulling up even harder*)   Again!

Young Saleem (*standing on toenails now*)   Aiee sir an animal an animal please sir aiee!

Zagallo   (*pulling up harder, higher*)   Once more!

Young Saleem *suddenly falls to the floor. Silence.*

Sonny   Sir, you pulled his hair out, sir.

Boys (*cacophony*)   Look sir, blood/He's bleeding sir/please sir shall I take him to the nurse?/Snotnose is a bal-die! Sniffer's got a map-face!

And music.

The Cathedral School Social. **Young Saleem** *wraps his head in a bandage – isolated in the throng of box-stepping, Mexican-hatting, boys and girls dancing.*

Masha Miovic (*golden-haired, prominent-chested fourteen-year-old*) Hey, Saleem, isn't it? Hey, man, what happened to you?

Young Saleem *stares at this vision.*

Masha My name is Masha Miovic. I've met your sister, Jamila.

Young Saleem (*stuttering*) I know . . . I know your name. You're the school's breaststroke champion. You are Jamila's heroine.

Masha (*straightening* **Young Saleem**'s *tie*) And I know your name, so that's fair.

Glandy Keith *and* **Fat Perce** *drool enviously.*

Masha So what about your bandage?

Young Saleem (*straight-backed, shoulders back, as deep a voice as he can muster*) It's nothing. A sporting accident. Would you like to . . . to dance?

Masha Okay. But don't try any smooching.

Young Saleem *takes the floor with* **Masha**: *the Mexican hat; box-stepping. The dancing ends.*

Young Saleem Would you care for a stroll, you know, in the quad?

Masha Miovic Well, yah, just for a sec; but hands off, okay?

Young Saleem *and* **Masha** *take the air.*

Young Saleem Man, this is fine. This is the life.

Out of the shadows of the quadrangle step **Glandy Keith** *and* **Fat Perce**, *giggling, blocking their path.*

Glandy Keith *and* **Fat Perce**   Hee hee.

Fat Perce   Hoo hoo, Masha, hoo hoo. Some date you got there.

Young Saleem   Shut up, you.

Glandy Keith   You wanna know how he got his war-wound, Mashy?

Fat Perce   Hee hoo ha.

Masha   Don't be *crude*; he got it in a sporting accident!

Fat Perce *and* **Glandy Keith** *almost fall over with mirth.*

Fat Perce   Zagallo pulled his hair out in class! Hee hoo.

Glandy Keith   Snotnose is a bal-die!

Fat Perce *and* **Glandy Keith**   Sniffer's got a map-face!

Masha   Saleem, they're being so rude about you!

Young Saleem   Yes, ignore them.

Masha   You aren't going to let them get away with it?

Pause. Then **Young Saleem** *gives a yell and kicks* **Glandy Keith** *in the groin.*

Young Saleem   Yeeaaa! Take that, Glandy!

He swivels round kung-fu style, and lets **Fat Perce** *have the same treatment.*

And you, Fishwala!

Masha   Hey man, pretty good!

But **Fat Perce** *and* **Glandy Keith** *are picking themselves up.*

Young Saleem   Oh, Lord.

Young Saleem *turns, and runs.*

Masha   Where are you running, little hero?

Young Saleem *has dashed into the nearest classroom –* **Fat Perce** *and* **Glandy Keith** *follow him in and chase him around the desks.* **Young Saleem** *makes for the door again – grabs the door with his right hand and tries to open it –* **Fat Perce** *hurls himself against the door and it slams shut. A thud.* **Masha** *looks down at the floor outside the classroom – sees the tip of* **Young Saleem***'s middle finger – and faints.* **Young Saleem** *holds out his hand: red liquid spurts where his middle finger should be.*

Breach Candy Hospital. **Mary Pereira** *and* **Jamila** *are there.* **Amina** *and* **Ahmed** *are with their son.*

Amina   O God preserve us, my little Piece-of-the-Moon, what have they done to you?

Doctor   Accidents will happen. Boys will be.

Amina   What kind of school? I'm here with my son's finger in pieces. Not good enough. No, sir.

Doctor   Mrs Sinai, your blood group please? The boy has lost blood. A transfusion may be necessary.

Amina   I am A; but my husband, O. Both rhesus positive.

Doctor   And the boy?

Amina *sobs and shakes her head.*

Doctor   Don't worry. A very quick test.

Ahmed   And the bit. Has anyone got the bit?

Doctor (*to* **Young Saleem**)   Just sit there, son, I'll give you a local anaesthetic.

Amina *makes to protest.*

Doctor   No, madam, he's in shock, total anaesthesia would be impossible, all right, son, just hold your hand up and still, help him nurse, and it'll be over in a jiffy.

Pause. A jiffy or two later.

Have you got a second, Mrs Sinai . . . Mrs Sinai, the blood groups: you are sure? O and A? A and O? And positive, both of you?

Amina   Positive. Positive.

Doctor   . . . Excuse me, madam, but he is . . . your son? Not adopted or similar?

Amina   But of course you must believe me, Doctor; my God, *of course he is our son*!

Doctor   Mrs Sinai . . .

Amina   I don't understand. A doctor's daughter, and I don't understand.

Ahmed   I should have known. Where am I in that face? That nose? I should have known.

Amina   Janumplease. Ibegyou. No, what are you saying. Of course you are the father . . . I swear! Iswearonmymother'shead. Now shh . . . he is . . .

Young Saleem   Abba . . .

Ahmed (*towering above his son on the hospital bed*)   Get him out of my sight.

Ahmed *storms out.*

Amina (*following*)   No, janum, I won't let you believe such things about me! I'll kill myself . . .

Ahmed *slaps* **Amina** *off-stage.*

Young Saleem *flops down, his head in his hands. He is left alone in the hospital bed. The noise of the voices mounts in his head. He puts his hands to his ears.*

Children's voices (*whispering*)   Saleem! Saleem!

Young Saleem   What's happening?

Children's voices   Listen to us! To us! Saleem!

Young Saleem (*afraid*)   What's happened?

Children's voices (*hissing*)   Saleem! Listen!

Young Saleem   Abba! Amma! There's a noise. I'm hearing voices!

Children's voices   Saleem!

Young Saleem (*loudly*)   Who are you? Get out of my head! Get out!

We discern a cluster of **Children** *– on stage, on film.*

Children   Saleem! We're here! Saleem!

Young Saleem   Go away! I don't know you!

Parvati   Saleem! We're like you! Born like you!

Young Saleem   What do you mean, born like me?

Parvati   At midnight.

He understands. He stands up.

Young Saleem   You mean . . . that midnight? Really? All of you!

Parvati   Midnight's Children.

Young Saleem   Then I'm not alone. I'm not alone! I'm not alone!!!

PART TWO

Voices – Midnight's Children – **Saleem***'s face picked out in the dim light.*

Pickle factory.

Saleem, *disconsolate, head bowed, slumped.*

Music: like an eerie dream.

Wee Willie Winkie, *hammer in hand, passes a couple of cripple beggars and approaches his sleeping son* **Shiva,** *guiltily. He pulls back the sack from the boy's legs, exposing his massive knees. Shaking,* **Winkie** *raises the hammer high above his head, about to bring it down on* **Shiva***'s knees.*

Winkie God forgive me.

At that precise moment, **Shiva***'s eyes pop open. Blackout. Then:*

Pickle factory. **Saleem** *wakes up with a start. The door opens. It is* **Padma***. She's back. She goes to put her arms on his shoulders. He leans back against her body and sighs deeply, happily.*

Padma O, mister, what to say? I have come back to make you better.

She produces a delicious-looking thali of food and sprinkles herbs on it, then presents it, with green Braganza Pickles chutney, to **Saleem***. She looks on fondly as he eats.*

Food is good? Enjoying it?

Saleem Very much.

Padma *kisses his head.* **Saleem** *smiles.*

Saleem Mmm . . .

Padma I went to a holy man in the hills. He gave me one secret herb with which your manhood can be awakened from its sleep.

Saleem *pauses: he begins to look a bit peculiar.*

Padma Then I ground the herb in water and said: 'Thou potent and lusty herb! Give my Mr Saleem thy power.'

Saleem *looking woozy now.*

Padma 'O herb, thou hast powers of Indra and the lusty force of beasts.' And this I have put in your food! Soon you will be well!

Padma *beams.* **Saleem** *collapses, unconscious, face first into the thali.*

Film.

Newsreel Announcer Radical reorganisation of India's family of states! Bombay State to be chopped in two! Relations with Pakistan 'severely strained', PM reveals! England's cricketers are here! India welcomes the famous MCC!

Pickle factory. **Saleem** *is delirious (in bed).*

Saleem Radical reorganisation of family . . . chopped in two . . . they sent me away . . . Pakistan . . . yes, relations, strained . . . yes, yes . . . the MCC . . .

Padma (*panic-stricken*) Oh, mister! What to say? Everything is my own poor fault!

Saleem The Midnight's Children Conference . . . yes, yes. My personal MCC . . .

Padma (*despairs*) You and your stories! All day, all night! Stop some time, how can it hurt?

Saleem (*shaking his head, taking her hand*) Padma, my Lotus Goddess. Padma, Guardian of Life . . .

Padma (*bemused, but pleased*)   Such fancy talk.

Saleem   Let me tell it, Padma. How I was banished from my own home.

Amina, Jamila, Ahmed (*whisky in hand*), *and* **Mary Pereira.**

Amina   Oh, my boy . . . my little Piece-of-the-Moon . . .

Jamila   So. You're off, then.

Young Saleem   Yes. No more shoe-burning.

Jamila *tuts.*

Young Saleem (*with feeling*)   I'll miss you.

Jamila (*without feeling*)   See you, then.

Ahmed *implacable, thunderous.*

Saleem   I was sent to stay with my auntie Emerald in Pakistan, the Land of the Pure.

Journey: ship, the blast of its horn as it docks – the train – the car with the army chauffeur – film: unglamorous late-1950s Pakistan, contrasting with earlier images of Bombay – until:

Rawalpindi. Northern Pakistan. **Zulfikar**'s *house.* **Emerald, Zulfikar** (*now a General*) *and their son* **Zia** *greet him.*

Zulfikar   Welcome, little hero.

Emerald   Saleem. Right-o. This is your cousin Zia. He'll show you the ropes.

Young Saleem   Yes. Emerald Auntie.

He puckers for a kiss – she waves him away.

Emerald   Understand me. My sister asks a favour, I can't refuse. Whatever my personal inclinations. She wants me to take you in, I have taken you in. Keep a clean nose, don't annoy General Zulfikar, don't break the antiques, and we'll get along.

She leaves.

Young Saleem Pakistan. What a complete dump!

Zia What did you do to get kicked out of India?

Young Saleem I hear you still wet your bed.

Zia, *humiliated, withdraws.*

Saleem Despite my bravado, I missed home.

The song of **Mary Pereira**
  Anything you want to be you can be;
  You can be just what-all you want . . .

Young Saleem *sleeps* – **Parvati** *appears on film on the screen.*

Parvati (*on screen*) Saleem . . .

Young Saleem *rouses.*

Young Saleem Who *are* you?

Parvati (*now appearing on stage*) I'm Parvati-the-witch.

Young Saleem A real witch?

Parvati (*proudly*) I was born seven seconds after midnight. My magic isn't any trick.

Young Saleem Show me some, then.

Parvati Not now. Maybe one day.

Shiva, *on screen, then on stage, shoulders her aside.*

Shiva I know you, rich boy.

Young Saleem (*amazed*) Shiva? Wee Willie Winkie's boy?

Shiva How are you doing this? Bringing us here? It's damn good.

Young Saleem What happened to your father? He stopped coming round.

Shiva I killed him.

65

Young Saleem   You murdered him?

Shiva   He lost his singing voice. He wanted me to beg. He wanted to break my knees because cripples do better business. So I grabbed his neck between my knees, and squeezed. I am number one. I am Warrior! The King!

Young Saleem   That's horrible.

Shiva *snorts, in disgust.*

Young Saleem   Horrible! Horrible!

On both stage and screen, other children appear.

Saleem   In my years of exile, I finally came to know Midnight's Children. One thousand and one of them were born in that hour after midnight on August the fifteenth, 1947. Malnutrition, disease, misfortune subtracted four hundred and twenty. That left five hundred and eighty-one. Five hundred and eighty-one miracles . . . the closer to midnight our birth-times, the greater were our gifts . . . those children born in the last seconds were – to be frank – little more than circus freaks . . . But children born in the first minute of all – for these children the hour had reserved the highest talents men had ever dreamed of.

Gujarati Girl   I can heal wounds by touching them!

Assamese Boy   I forget nothing!

Bengali Boy   I can eat metal!

Goan Girl   I can multiply fish!

Vindhyan Boy   I can make myself very small . . . or very big . . .

Kashmiri Girl   If I enter water, I change sex!

Sharp-Tongued Girl (*sadly*)   When I make my words sharp, they cut people to ribbons.

Jalna Boy   I can make gold.

Madrasi Boy   Watch me! Watch me fly!

Young Saleem *turns to* **Parvati** *but she is gone. So too is* **Shiva**, *his contemptuous laughter hanging in the air.*

Pickle factory. **Padma** *applying cold compresses to* **Saleem**'*s fevered brow.*

Padma   O, mister. Such a high fever. You don't know what crazy things it's been making you say.

Saleem *pulls himself up in his bed.*

Saleem (*incensed*)   No! No! It's not the fever! This isn't delirium. Padma, listen to me. You can think of us as freaks if you want. Maybe we were freaks. But this isn't make-believe. It happened. It was real.

Two of us were born on the stroke of midnight. Saleem and Shiva, Shiva and Saleem, nose and knees and knees and nose . . . to Shiva, the hour had given the gifts of war . . . and to me, the greatest talent of all: the ability to look into the hearts and minds of men.

There; now I've said it. Nothing less than the literal, by-the-hairs-of-my-mother's-head truth. That is who I was – who we were . . .

And what happened next really happened, too. It may seem far-fetched, but it was real, too. Really. Truly.

Rawalpindi.

Zia (*to* **Young Saleem**)   It's the C-in-C. And most of the top brass. Top secret. Something's up. Pretty scary, man.

The **Top Brass**. *A dinner.* **Zia** *and* **Saleem** *are lurking.*

C-in-C   Twelve months ago, I spoke to all of you. Give the politicians one year – is that not what I said?

Heads nod; murmurs of assent. **Zia** *and* **Saleem** *attempt to leave.*

C-in-C   No, stay, young men. It is your future after all.

That year has elapsed; the situation remains intolerable. Corruption, impurity in all quarters.

Stern, statesmanlike expressions. Jaws are set, eyes gaze keenly into the future.

Tonight, therefore, by my order, Martial Law has been imposed. The Constitution is abrogated! (*increasingly stentorian*) Central and Provincial legislatures are dissolved! Political parties are abolished! General Zulfikar!!! (*suddenly conversational*) Our cordial host will map out procedure.

Zulfikar   Thank you sir. (*to* **Zia**) Zia! Up here, boy.

Zia *wets his pants. In cold fury* **Zulfikar** *hurls him from the room.*

Zulfikar   Pimp! Woman! Coward! Homosexual! Hindu!

His eyes settle on **Young Saleem.**

(*to* **Young Saleem**) Save the honour of the family. Redeem me from the incontinence of my son. (*aloud*) You, boy! You want to come up here and help me?

Young Saleem *steps up to the table. Throughout this speech, he shifts the salt cellars and bowls of chutney, etc., on behalf of his uncle* **Zulfikar.**

Zulfikar   How to make a revolution: this mustard jar is Company A occupying Head Post Office; there are two pepper pots surrounding a serving spoon, which means Company B has seized the airport. Condiments, cutlery capture empty biriani dishes with water glasses, stationing salt cellars, on guard, around water jugs.

C-in-C   Very good, Zulfikar; good show. Except one table ornament remains uncaptured: that cream jug in solid silver.

Zulfikar   In our table-top coup, sir, it represents the Head of State, President Iskander Mirza. (*to* **Young Saleem,** *whispering*) Come on, sonny, it's time you got a taste of the real thing!

Young Saleem   Where are we going, Zulfy – uncle?

Zulfikar   Wait and see.

With **Soldiers,** *they march along half-lit corridors, bursting into a dark room with a shaft of moonlight spotlighting a four-poster bed, draped in a mosquito net.*

Mirza (*waking*)   What the hell is going . . .

Zulfikar *forces the tip of his long-barrelled revolver between* **Mirza**'s *teeth.*

Mirza   Mmff –

Zulfikar   Shut up. Come with us. Turn. Quick march!

Zulfikar *points the pistol into* **Mirza**'s *buttocks.*

Mirza   For God's sake, be careful; that thing has the safety off!

Zulfikar   Mr President. You're a lucky man. It's only exile for you.

Pickle factory.

Saleem   'Only exile . . . !' In my exile in Pakistan, I learned about power. I overthrew a government. And I learned about loneliness. Four years with no friends – except for Midnight's Children.

Young Saleem, *with* **Parvati** *and* **Shiva,** *sits before the* **Children.**

Shiva   Gangs need gang bosses, rich kid. Now, me, I've been running a gang in Matunga. Everyone does what I say or they get the old squeeze from the knees. And these knees: boy, they can squeeze.

Young Saleem   It's me who's doing this, Shiva . . . (*addressing the whole gathering*) It's me that's bringing you all together in my head. Without me there'd be no Conference at all!

Parvati He's right. It's his party, yaar. Let him be.

Shiva *retreats*.

Young Saleem Okay, then. Let's get started. We need a programme. A plan. We must think what we are for.

Bengali Boy We should all get together and form a community, no? What would we need from anyone else?

Individualist Child You say 'we'; but we together are unimportant; what matters is that each of us has a gift to use for his or her own good.

Filial Duty Child However we can help our father-mother, that is what it is for us to do.

Revolutionary Child No, we must show all kids that it is possible to get rid of parents! Infant revolution!

Capitalist Child Just think what business we could do! How rich, Allah, we could be!

Altruistic Child Our country needs gifted people; we must ask the government how it wishes to use our skills.

Science Child We must allow ourselves to be studied.

Religious Child Let us declare ourselves to the world, so that all may glory in God.

Coward Child O heavens, we must stay secret, just think what they will do to us, stone us for witches or what-all!

Women's Lib Child A declaration of women's rights!

Untouchable Child Improve the lot of the untouchables!

Shiva Be quiet! Listen to me. They can't stop us, yaar! We can bewitch, and fly, and read minds, and make gold and fishes. We can change sex and vanish through mirrors and make them fall in love with us . . . How will they be able to fight?

Young Saleem I'm talking about destiny.

Shiva And I'm talking about taking over! About staging our own coup. I'm talking about living like generals . . . like kings!

All the **Children** *cheer – much to* **Young Saleem***'s despair.*

Young Saleem We are supposed to be something new.

Emerald *at her boudoir, trying on, yes, emeralds – necklaces, earrings, rings, chokers, bracelets. A knock on the door.*

Emerald Come.

Young Saleem *enters.*

Emerald Just fasten this, darling.

From behind her, **Young Saleem** *fastens her necklace.*

Love you. Do you mind?

Young Saleem *puts an emerald choker around her neck.*

Emerald Such a helpful boy. I told your ma, you must have him back, whatever the problem was. She's been on your side all along. Been working on your pater for yonks. He's bound to relent soon. Anyway, you've been here *quite* a while, haven't you? Best you were off. I've arranged everything. You're going back to Bombay, my dear. Home! . . .

In his excitement, **Young Saleem** *has been clumsy.*

Arré, madman, are you trying to strangle me?

He lets the choker fall to the floor.

Idiot! Out of my sight!

Young Saleem *flees.* **Emerald** *turns to admire her jewels.*

Emerald I must say: life is good.

Film: aerial view as **Young Saleem** *flies back to Bombay – to the accompaniment of a 1962 soundtrack.*

Young Saleem Back to Bom! Back to Bom!

*But it's not his parents, just **Uncle Hanif** who greets him at the airport.*

Hanif   Hey, big fellow! Mister wrestler! You look fine.

Young Saleem (*looking around him*)   Uncle Hanif . . . my parents . . . they didn't come?

Hanif (*an uncly arm round his shoulder*)   Soon, my boy. Soon. But your ayah, Mary – she is waiting to greet you.

Hanif *and* **Pia**'*s apartment* – **Mary Pereira** *is there to greet* **Young Saleem**.

Mary   My little Piece-of-the-Moon! (*She hugs him.*) But so thin! They didn't feed you properly? Sit down. I have steak! Chips! Ice-cream soda! Banana split! And your favourite chutney as promised.

Young Saleem *grins in spite of himself.*

Young Saleem   The green one?

Mary   Green as grasshoppers!

Mary *exits, and as she does so,* **Pia** *enters – she is still adorably beautiful, flirtatious: as coquettish as a true Bombay movie goddess.*

Pia   Come here, don't be shy. Kiss me at once.

He does, trying to avert his eyes from her impossible breasts.

Mmm. Well, you've grown up. I hope you haven't forgotten your auntie Pia.

Young Saleem   Auntie, of course not.

During **Pia**'*s speech,* **Mary** *returns with a tray of food and green chutney.*

Pia   Thank God! One fan at least. After *Lovers of Kashmir*, who was a bigger star? Nobody; not one person! What to do? Public is fickle.

Hanif   Not now, Pia. Let the boy arrive at least.

Pia Your uncle is no use. Nothing but social-conscience dramas these days. My advice, he ignores. Arré, make heroes heroic! Make your villains villainous! Put in a little comedy, a little dance number for your Pia. No, no. 'Not realistic.' So, flop, flop, flop.

Hanif Pia.

Pia And you know what he is writing now? About . . . the Ordinary Life of a Pickle Factory!

Hanif Pia, this damn country has been dreaming for five thousand years. It's about time it started waking up. Princes! Demons! Gods and heroes! The Bombay film is a temple of illusions. I am a high priest of reality. I am writing the story of a pickle factory created, run and worked in entirely by women. There are long scenes describing the formation of a trade union; there are detailed descriptions of the pickling process.

Pia Maybe just one love scene? What do you think, village people are going to give their rupees to see women pickling Alfonsos?

Hanif This is a film about work, not kissing. And nobody pickles Alfonsos. You must use cheaper mangoes with bigger stones.

Pia Saleem has suffered. He knows what it is to lose those who used to love you. Isn't it, Saleem?

Hanif Pia, control yourself.

Pia Homi Catrack would give you a big budget, but your brow is too high, isn't it? Leave me in peace now. If you hear nothing, it is because my heart is broken and I am dead.

She slams out and into the bedroom – a terrific exit.

Hanif Saleem . . . your mother never wanted to lose you. But Ahmed bhai . . . you are old enough to understand . . . with his drink problem, you know . . . her life has been very hard also. Be forgiving if you can. She has been fighting for you.

Young Saleem   Will she come?

Hanif   Let's hope so. Everything will be tickety-boo. Just wait and see.

Hanif *exits.*

Mary *sings* **Young Saleem** *to sleep.*

The song of **Mary Pereira**
    Anything you want to be you can be;
    You can be just what-all you want . . .

Later: **Young Saleem** *asleep.* **Pia** *enters.*

Pia   Saleem. Are you awake?

Young Saleem   Auntie?

She joins him under his light quilt.

Pia   Can you keep a secret? Will you do something just for me?

Young Saleem   Of course.

A movement under the quilt.

Pia (*whispering*)   Give this to the film magnate, Homi Catrack. Into his hand. Tell nobody.

Saleem   For many years she had been his fancy woman and now he has tired of her charms. He has somebody else now.

Pia   Homi Catrack. (*a tragedienne's wail and flail*) Hai! Hai, hai! *Ai*-hai-hai! Traitor Homi! Heartless friend Homi! How can you think that Lila Sabarmati is better than me?

Young Saleem *and* **Pia** *grasp one another –* **Pia** *thrashes about.*

Pia   O! O God, O God, O!

The thrashing about could be misconstrued as sexual – hips grinding and so on – and **Young Saleem** *misconstrues and touches* **Pia***'s yearned-for breast – she wallops his face.*

Young Saleem   Yaaaouuuu!

Pia   *Badmaash*! A family of maniacs and perverts, woe is me, what woman ever suffered so badly.

Pia *exits.*

Young Saleem *is being taken home by his mother,* **Amina.** **Mary** *is with them, too.*

Amina   O child, with your face like the sun coming out. Oh, forgive me. Terrible things happen in this life and you don't know how.

Young Saleem (*embracing her*)   Amma. Amma.

Amina   You're a man, now. A fine young man. Be good with your father; he is not happy these days.

Ahmed (*whisky in hand, glaring at* **Saleem**)   That damn nose. Drip, drip. One of these days . . .

Saleem (*to* **Padma**)   Everything was different when I got back. And everything was the same. Ish.
Mary hadn't dared to go to confession for fifteen years. Eyeslice was still there –

Eyeslice   Saleem, yaar!

Saleem   And Hairoil –

Hairoil   Nice to see you again.

Saleem   – but their mother, Lila, turned out to be the traitor wife who stole the philandering playboy Homi Catrack from my traitor aunt Pia.

Lila Sabarmati*, champagne glass in hand, chin-chins with* **Homi Catrack.**

Lila   Just imagine how I have been confined all these years. A woman like me, stuck with a Navy commander's salary. But now I am blossoming. Opening, like a flower. For you . . . oh, Homi.

Saleem   Lila Sabarmati. Mother of my old chums Eyeslice and Hairoil. Wife of the highest flyer in the Indian Navy. While Commander Sabarmati was at sea on manoeuvres, Lila and Homi were performing certain manoeuvres of their own . . .

And as for my sister, Jamila . . .

Jamila *appears like a vision of perfect femininity – no longer the tomboy.*

Young Saleem   Wow!

Jamila   What do you mean, 'wow!'?

(*sings*)
   'Every time you say goodbye I sigh a little', *etc.*

Saleem   She was a tomboy no more.

Jamila   Poor brother.

A phone rings in Buckingham Villa.

Saleem   And the phone didn't seem to stop ringing.

Amina (*on the phone*)   No. No truck company. Wrong number. (*quiet*) Where? When?

Music: like a film soundtrack.

Pioneer Café.

Nadir *and* **Amina** *in the distance, as if in a film seen from* **Saleem**'s *point of view.*

Saleem   Once upon a time there was an underground husband who fled, leaving loving messages of divorce. Nadir Khan. Now Nadir the Red, official candidate of the official Communist Party of India (Marxist-Leninist).

Nadir *and* **Amina**'s *hands stretch towards each other's – but jerk away without touching, like the censor's cuts. Then* **Amina** *lifts her glass of Lovely Lassi and kisses it, and passes it to* **Nadir**, *who kisses it too.*

Saleem So life imitated bad art; and my uncle Hanif's invention, the Indirect Kiss, arrived at the Pioneer Café.

He turns away distressed.

Young Saleem How could she how could she how could she?

I began to cut pieces out of newspapers.

On the screen we see the headlines, etc., and the key letters picked out in bold:

From GOAN LIBERATION **COM**MITTEE LAUNCHES SATYAGRAHA CAMPAIGN, I extracted the letters 'COM'.

SPEAKER OF E-PAK ASSEMBLY DECLARED **MAN**IAC – 'MAN'.

'DER'? – NEHRU CONSI**DER**S RESIGNATION AT CONGRESS ASSEMBLY.

And so on. Cutting up history to suit my nefarious purposes, I seized on: **WHY** INDIRA GHANDI IS CONGRESS PRESIDENT NOW for a 'WHY'; but I refused to be tied exclusively to politics.

DOES YOUR CHEWING GUM LOSE ITS FLAVOUR? BUT P.K. KEEPS ITS SAVOUR!

MOHUN BAGAN CENTRE-FORWARD TAKES **WIFE**.

The masthead of the **SUNDAY** BLITZ gave me 'SUNDAY'. Now I found myself just one word short. Events in East Pakistan provided me with my finale: FURNITURE HURLING SLAYS DEPUTY E-PAK SPEAKER: **MOURNING** PERIOD DECLARED.

I needed a question mark: AFTER NEHRU, WHO?

On screen, made up of the anonymous newspaper clippings.

COMMANDER SABARMATI
WHY DOES YOUR WIFE GO TO COLABA
CAUSEWAY ON SUNDAY MORNING?

Saleem (*of* **Amina**) – *pour encourager les autres.*

Commander Sabarmati *reads the note at breakfast with* **Lila.**

Lila (*uninterested*)   Anything in the post?

She pecks him lightly on the head as she passes.

Sabarmati   Nothing.

The following scenes run simultaneously in the style of a 1960s Bombay romance melodrama.

Sabarmati, *face grimly set, shaves meticulously.*

Lila *prepares herself for* **Homi.**

Lila *sings first verse of 'Oh What a Beautiful Morning'.*

Sabarmati *brushes his well-oiled hair with two hairbrushes.*

Lila *adjusts herself in the mirror.*

Lila *sings chorus of 'Oh What a Beautiful Morning'.*

Sabarmati *finishes buttoning up his full dress whites and reaches for his cap – and his gun. And leaves.*

Homi *enters and embraces* **Lila.** *They smooch. The doorbell rings. The door is answered by* **Lila** *– it's* **Sabarmati.** *He shoots her twice in the stomach at point-blank range. She falls backwards. He goes past her and finds* **Homi** (*on the toilet*). **Sabarmati** *shoots* **Homi** *in the genitals, the heart, the right eye.*

Film: on screen: a newspaper whirls towards us. Headline: SUPREME COURT: SABARMATI GUILTY!!!

Buckingham villa – **Amina** *reads the newspaper in shock.*

Young Saleem   I did this, Ammi. I made this happen.

Amina   Don't be mad, Saleem. How could you?

Young Saleem   The anonymous note. I sent it.

Amina (*horrified*)   Why, son? Such a terrible deed . . .

Young Saleem (*bursts out*)   Because of you. To show you . . .

Amina (*colouring*)   Me? What have I done? To show me what?

Young Saleem   Amma, don't go to see other men!!! Enough glass-kissery, okay??? Enough Nadir!!!

He flees. **Amina** *is left in shock. She picks up the phone and dials.*

Nadir's voice   Hullo, yes?

Amina   This is a wrong number. Please believe what I am telling you. A wrong, wrong number for you to call.

Nadir's voice   But you called me.

Amina   Can't you hear me? Just never call this household, this family. Never again.

She hangs up. Her shoulders silently shake. **Young Saleem** *watches from a distance.*

Young Saleem   However, in killing Homi Catrack, I was to kill my uncle, too. When he learned of Pia's betrayal, Hanif took himself up to the roof of his apartment block and stepped out into the evening sea breeze. He frightened the beggars so much when he fell that they gave up pretending to be blind and ran away yelling. In death as in life, Uncle Hanif espoused the cause of truth and put illusion to flight.

The **Midnight's Children** *appear.*

Shiva   So your uncle's dead. Who cares? One Muslim less.

Some **Children** *murmur their assent, to* **Young Saleem**'s *shock.*

Shiva   You think all the Hindus here love the Muslims? The Muslims love the Sikhs? The Brahmins love the untouchables? The fair-skinned Northerners love the Southern blackies? The rich guys like beggar girls? The –

Young Saleem   What's all this? High-caste, low-caste – Hindu-Muslim – rich-poor – that's not for us! We can find a . . . a new way.

79

Some **Children** *jeer.*

Shiva You're a good one to talk. Sister-fucking uncle murderer!

The **Children** *are hostile.* **Shiva** *pushes* **Young Saleem** *in the chest;* **Young Saleem** *staggers back.* **Shiva** *circles him.*

Shiva Rich boy. (*another shove*) Uncle-murderer. (*another one*) Hell's bells, cucumber-nose. (*another shove*) I'm sick of your Conference.

One final push – a moment of violence – and they all exit.

Saleem Homi Catrack. Dead. Lila Sabarmati. Dead. Commander Sabarmati, jailed – our little world had been smashed. And developers were buying up Methwold's Estate, to knock it down and build a giant skyscraper.

The Aziz family gather for forty days of mourning Hanif: **Aadam, Reverend Mother, Alia, Zulfikar, Emerald** *and their wet-pants son* **Zia. Ahmed, Amina, Jamila, Young Saleem, Mary Pereira, Pia** *– all in funeral gear. They cover everything in dust sheets. Dust falls throughout the scene.*

My family gathered to mourn Uncle Hanif, in dust and in silence. From Karachi my aunt Alia –

Jamila (*to* **Young Saleem**) Imagine, Abba was going to marry her once; she could have been our mummy. Lucky for us, Amma came along instead.

Saleem And from Agra came my grandparents – Reverend Mother, and old Aadam Aziz.

Reverend Mother To marry an actress, whatsitsname, my son made his bed in the gutter. She made him drink alcohol, eat pig. She shouldn't do this actressy thing. Why to do such shameless behaviour? Work, yes, you girls have modern ideas, but to dance naked on the screen! That is proper work?! That woman, whatsitsname, didn't I tell you about her? My son, Allah, he could have been anything, but no, whatsitsname, she must make him ruin his life; he must jump off a roof, whatsitsname, to be free of her. Until that woman shows my son's memory some respect, whatsitsname, until she takes out a wife's true tears, no food will pass my lips.

A look passes between the Aziz family who have been here before . . .

It is shame and scandal, whatsitsname, how she sits with kajal instead of tears in her eyes!

Through the dust sheets, shrouded in dust, comes the **Ghost of Joseph D'Costa.** **Mary** *whimpers.*

Mary No . . . don't come back, Joe . . . don't come back. I can't tell them. I can't.

Aadam Who are you?

Joe You can see me? God Almighty!

Aadam Did you say God . . . ?

Joe You can hear me too? Jesus! God!

Aadam (*clutching his heart*) Jesus . . .

Reverend Mother (*bewildered*) What's this? Are you sick?

Aadam *clutches his chest.*

Joe (*gobsmacked*) This isn't right.

Joe *retreats and disappears.* **Mary** *whimpers. Everyone stares at* **Aadam** *clutching his heart.*

Aadam Where are you going? Come back here! Give me back my son! Give him back!! I knew it. He wasn't worth believing in, after all.

Aadam *falls to the floor.* **Reverend Mother** *lumbers to his side.* **Pia** *starts to cry.*

Family tableau – **Aadam**'s *deathbed scene.*

Saleem Methwold's Estate was dying, and so was my grandfather.

Aadam *dies.*

Amina   He's dead.

Which, what with the appearance of **Joe's Ghost** *as well, prompts* **Mary** *to confess all to the family about* **Saleem's** *birth.*

Mary   It's all my fault. It is me to blame. It's a secret which has been hidden since he was born – when I swapped the name tags – it was Joe who inspired me, because of his politics and all – and now his ghost won't rest until I tell the tale – (*to* **Ahmed**) God forgive me, but I changed them, sir. (*To* **Amina**) I did it for my Joe, madam. God forgive me, I will burn in hell. He is Winkie and Vanita's boy. I will go, I will go now, sahib, only this is a good boy, sahib, you must not send him away, sahib, he is your own . . . O, you boy with your face like the sun coming out, O Saleem my Piece-of-the-Moon, you must know that your father was Winkie and your mother is also dead . . .

Padma (*blubbing*)   O, mister. Too sad!

Saleem   Come on now, it's an old story. And she's wrong. My father was Methwold.

Padma   What's happened to her, that Mary?

Mary *runs out of the house.*

Saleem   You ask her!

Padma   How? How can I ask her?

Ahmed's *red-rimmed eyes swivel to* **Young Saleem.**

Ahmed   You . . .

Amina (*steely*)   He will not go.

All eyes turn to her.

Once before I did not want him to go, and he was sent. This time I will not allow it. He is my child. Love is not only

82

born, but made. I have loved him for fifteen years. I will not stay if he goes.

Ahmed (*to* **Amina**) You will not stay?

Silence.

Then we will all go.

Amina (*not understanding*) What are you saying?

Ahmed (*shrugs, drinks his whisky*) This country is finished. Better to start again. In Pakistan.

Amina (*incredulous*) You want to go to Pakistan?

Ahmed We can stay with Alia till we build a house. And the high-rise johnnies can have this cursed house and blow it to pieces.

Jamila's *turn to be upset.*

Jamila We're going to leave our home? Leave India? And go to Pakistan? Pakistan is a dump!

Alia Young lady. You'd better change your tune. None of your smart Indian ways! In Pakistan the youngsters fear God. They respect their elders. They demand something you Bombay kids maybe don't understand.

Jamila What, Auntie?

Alia Purity. Purity of the heart. Purity of word and deed. Purity of faith. It is the Land of the Pure.

Reverend Mother I also will go to Pakistan. To the land of the pure and away from this land with too many gods. I will set up a Petrol Pump. (*to* **Pia**) Daughter. You will come with me.

Pia Me? Me going in for pumpery-shrumpery?

Young Saleem (*to* **Jamila**) Sis . . . it'll be okay . . . sis . . . We'll be together . . . I'll look after you, sister.

Jamila Didn't you hear? Are you deaf or what? I'm not your sister! I'm just not!

Young Saleem *bursts into paroxysms of sneezes.*

Ahmed   That damn nose. Come, Saleem.

Ear Nose Throat Clinic.

Two Orderlies *take* **Young Saleem** *gently by the arm.*

Young Saleem   No! You mustn't! You don't understand!

Young Saleem *sniffs violently, sneezes. Tries to escape, but is prevented from doing so by the* **Doctor, Nurse, Orderlies.**

Ahmed   Once and for all. About bloody time.

Young Saleem   Listen to me . . . you can't interfere with my head . . . you don't know what you're doing . . . please . . . please . . .

Nurse   Honestly, such a big baby, I never saw.

Doctor (*applying general-anaesthetic mask*)   Be a good fellow and count to ten.

Young Saleem   No please no . . . one two three . . . don't . . . four hundred million, five hundred, six . . . the numbers, marching . . . seven hundred million . . . eight hundred . . . nine . . .

Tick, tock.

The **Midnight's Children** *disappear.*

Blackout.

Young Saleem *is now recuperating in the hospital bed.* **Jamila** *by his side.*

Young Saleem   They've gone. The voices have gone for good.

Jamila (*caressing his head*)   Shh now. The gas makes people talk funny. Just shush now and take it easy.

(*Sings 'Paper Moon'.*)

Young Saleem   I'd lost Midnight's Children. But I was

discovering the astonishing delights of possessing, for the first time, a sense of smell.

Jamila *caresses his head.*

Saleem   And as we left Bombay for good, I could smell the sea air . . . the jasmine in her hair . . . and other smells, too. My father's disappointment . . . my mother's unhappiness . . . and love. I could smell love.

And **Jamila** *has continued to sing 'Paper Moon' along with soundtrack.*

Pickle factory. Silhouetted against venetian blinds is a woman, **Mrs Braganza,** *at a desk. The scene is lit so that her face remains in shadow.* **Padma** *enters.*

Mrs Braganza   Come, come, Padma. How is he today?

Padma   Oh, Mrs Braganza. Not so good, you know? Talking to himself and all.

Mrs Braganza   Take good care of him, Padma. Too much has happened to that poor gentleman. God willing, we will bring him back to good health.

Padma   Yes, madam.

Padma *leaves* **Mrs Braganza.**

Newsreel Announcer   Fifteen years after Partition, India and Pakistan's Kashmir dispute rumbles on. Usurped Pakistani territory or an integral part of India? Observers fear some flashpoint may spark full-scale hostilities!

Saleem   From our sea-crossing to the war . . . from my family's new beginning in Pakistan to its terrible end . . . it was just one thousand and one nights. For me, it was a too-soon-return to Pakistan. And I never forgave Karachi for not being Bombay. On my eighteenth birthday, I was given a Lambretta motor scooter; riding the city streets I couldn't get over the smell. And Lord! How it smelled. Not only camel-smells, car-smells, and motor-rickshaw fumes. But in

1965, the strongest smells were of power . . . and devotion
. . . and war.

Montage: footage/radio of build-up to war.

Saleem (*on scooter*)   My family's thousand and one nights
were almost up. Did we notice? No. We were too busy listening
to the now famous Jamila Singer. Yes. My sister. No, not my
sister. My love. Because by now it was clear to me I loved her.
That I had always loved her. And she wasn't my sister.

President*'s palace. Row of chairs on which sit the* **President**
(the **C-in-C** *from the table-top coup)*, **Zulfikar, Emerald,
Ahmed, Alia, Amina, Saleem** *and* **Army Top Brass,
Presidential Cronies.**

Audience   Ja-mi-la! Ja-mi-la!

*The small stage is dressed like a Pakistani flag: green-and-
white backdrop; a large silver crescent moon and star
suspended. House lights dim.*

Audience   Hurray! Hurray!

Jamila *comes on stage, wearing a head-to-foot burqa into
which a small hole has been cut, revealing her mouth.*

Saleem   Another perforated sheet.

Jamila *bows, makes the adab to the* **Top Brass,** *etc. then sits
on the crescent moon which subsequently rises into place.
She sings F.A. Faiz's ghazal 'Do not ask of me, my love' in
Urdu, a love song.*

Fantasy on film: **Jamila** *is not wearing the burqa but sitting
on the crescent moon Hollywood-style, one bare leg up, the
other dangling, and singing 'Paper Moon' in English.*

Then back to the burqad **Jamila** *on stage, singing 'Do not
ask of me, my love' in Urdu.*

The **Audience** *erupts in wild cheering. The* **Top Brass** *applaud.*

President   Jamila, daughter, you are truly Pakistan's angel.

Bulbul-e-Din – Nightingale of the Faith. The Voice of the Nation! War is coming. The enemy rises. But your voice will be a sword for purity; it will inspire our holy soldiers to victory!

Jamila   The President's will is the voice of my heart.

Back to **Alia**'s *house.* **Jamila** *is no longer burqad – beautiful, arrogant, a star high on her success, with* **Alia, Ahmed, Amina** *and* **Saleem**.

Saleem   You're really going? To sing for the soldiers, up north?

Jamila   They want me.

Saleem   But we're also from India, after all.

Jamila (*angry*)   You and your India, India. If they attack us, should we not defend ourselves?

Saleem   But Jamila, who is attacking? Who is defending? How to tell?

Jamila *flouncing off.*

Jamila   Arré, koi hai? Can't the star even get one drink or one samosa?

Saleem (*calling after her*)   Can I come with you?

Jamila   No!

Alia   A fine daughter, Ahmed bhai.

Alia *puts her arm through* **Ahmed**'s. **Amina** *stiffens.*

Amina (*kissing* **Saleem** *good night*)   I am going to bed.

They all retire.

Saleem *knocks on* **Jamila**'s *door.*

Saleem   Are you there?

Jamila   What do you want?

Saleem   I need to talk.

Jamila   Go away. I'm sleeping.

Saleem   No you're not. Jamila, please.

The door opens. **Jamila** *looks peevish.*

Jamila   Okay, okay. Better be good.

She is surrounded by flowers, gifts.

Men, huh. Can't resist what they can't see. The mouth without the face. Drives them crazy.

Saleem   That's what I wanted to talk about.

Jamila   About my fan club?

Saleem   About me. About you and me.

Jamila   Arré, Saleem, if this is about my tour I already told you no. For the thousand and first time. Stop acting like my brother or something.

Saleem   It's not about your tour.

Jamila   What then?

He just stands there.

What?

He can't say. But it's on his face.

Oh my God. That?

He nods dumbly. She slaps him as hard as she can. He does not move. She slaps him again. He does not move. She slaps him a third time.

It's disgusting. Disgusting. My own brother. For God's sake. Don't you know you're in this family on sufferance? And God how you make us suffer. You don't think if I told Amma she'd kick you out on your ear? On your fat nose? Chhi-chhi! Get out. Just don't ever talk to me again. Silence between us, understood? For the rest of your filthy life.

Saleem (to Padma) She wasn't my sister. She just wasn't.

That was the lowest point of my life. It seemed I could sink no lower. Jamila wanted nothing to do with me, of course. She was Pakistan's angel, and her mind was on higher things. Her duty was to serve the nation and the heroic boys in uniform.

Film: Newsreel. Battle of Lahore rages.

After all, she was the Voice of the Nation. The Nightingale of the Faith. So she headed for the front line in an army convoy, which had the added advantage of getting her far away from me. From the fate of our family, however, there was no escape; and when her truck stopped for petrol, there was only one petrol pump she could have stopped at. This was not coincidence. It was destiny.

Jamila (*wearing a burqa*) Auntie Pia! Auntie Pia! Over here!

Pia (*at the petrol pump in her overalls*) Jamila? Arré, Jamila, is it you in there?

Jamila It's me.

They embrace.

Pia Reverend Mother's in the office. These days her legs, you know. Strictly non-functional. Come, come. She is waiting. But what a star you became, my God. Bigger than I ever dreamed of!

Jamila (*to the* **Driver** *and* **Soldiers**) All of you! Fill up at this petrol pump! I am going to see my grandmother.

Driver Okay, Jamila Bibi.

In the office, **Reverend Mother** *sits cross-legged on a divan.* **Jamila** *sits at her feet, the face section of her burqa thrown back over her head.*

Reverend Mother Sing for me. Sing for me once before I die.

89

Pia You'll never die.

Jamila *sings 'Do not ask of me, my love' in Urdu.*

Montage: we hear the noise of planes overhead.

Tick, tock.

Saleem It was supposed to be about Kashmir, that war. But that's just what they said. It is my firm conviction that the hidden purpose of the Indo-Pakistani war of 1965 was the elimination of my benighted family from the face of the earth. My impurity condemned us all. We had to be cleansed.

Tick, tock.

Film: int. **Zulfikar's** *house.* **Emerald** *in her boudoir, wearing every piece of emerald jewellery she possesses, staring at herself in the mirror as the planes roar overhead.* **Zia** *stands in the corner, a wee-wee stain spreading across the front of his trousers. The room shakes – the roof falls in – the house collapses.*

Tick, tock.

Film: ext. Petrol Pump: the **Driver** *and* **Soldiers** *try to run from the gasoline, but they get in each other's way. The bombers bomb. Petrol flames billow upwards.* **Reverend Mother, Pia** *and* **Jamila** *wait for death amid the billowing flames.*

Tick, tock.

Film: ext. **Alia's** *house.* **Ahmed** *with* **Alia** *on one side,* **Amina** *on the other, waiting for death. The silver spittoon glinting nearby. The planes roar.*

Saleem *has stopped his scooter near the house. He looks up into the sky.*

Tick, tock,

Midnight.

The world explodes.

Alia's *house is utterly destroyed.*

While on screen each situation is a conflagration of death, **Saleem** *narrates the following event – we see the spittoon rising from the ruins as he does so. Film.*

Saleem   I look up: something which was hidden unseen for many years is circling in the night like a whirligig piece of the moon, twisting turning somersaulting down, the past plummeting towards me and a feeling at the back of my head followed by only a tiny but infinite moment of utter clarity before I am stripped of past present memory time shame and love, and all the Saleems go pouring out of me, from the baby who appeared in jumbo-sized front-page baby-snaps to the eighteen-year-old with his filthy dirty love, I am free now, beyond caring, restored to innocence and purity by my mother's wondrously worked inlaid with lapis lazuli silver spittoon.

The spittoon brains him and he's knocked out cold, unconscious, body prone on the floor of the stage.

On screen, we see **Saleem** *looking down at his prone body on the stage and then talking to us.*

Saleem (*on screen*)   Everything ended. Everything began again. I became a new person without family, no memory, no name. My worst fear, above all things: I feared absurdity.

Everybody I had known, my home, everything I knew was wiped out.

We didn't all die. In Pakistan, General Zulfikar lived to fight a bigger war.

I was alive but I didn't know who I was. For six years. And those six years later, I was plunged into another war: the war for Bangladesh.

Film: a Bombay-talkie-style close-up – a calendar ruffled by a breeze, its pages flying off in rapid succession to denote the passing of the years.

Oh yes, Padma, I'm not finished yet. There are next-attractions and coming-soons galore.

Padma *sniffs; wipes, dries eyes; breathes in deeply.*

Padma   O, your poor bomb-flattened clan! O, mister, this war business, kills the best and leaves the rest!

Caption: COMING SOON!

Saleem (*on screen*)   Coming soon, in 1970, was the election. Which a certain Mrs Indira Gandhi won in a landslide!

Caption: NEXT ATTRACTION.

Next attraction: Pakistan split in two. Pakistan, that strange bird, two wings without a body, broke apart.

Newsreel Announcer   Mrs Indira Gandhi takes power in a perilous hour! West Pakistan refuses to accept election results that give power to the East Wing's Sheikh Mujib!

On screen: an animated map showing the East and West Wings of Pakistan.

Mujib threatens to declare the East Wing the independent state of Bangladesh! West Pakistan's leaders cry havoc . . . and let loose the dogs of war!

Troop transport plane. **Pakistani Soldiers** *'frozen' mid-gesture, mid-speech.*

Saleem (*on screen*)   CUTIA – the Canine Unit for Tracking and Intelligence Activities. Elite troops, on their way to prevent the secession of Bangladesh. The acronym CUTIA, of course, means 'bitch'. Each pursuit team had its own tracker dog. Allow me to introduce three noble specimens of Pakistani soldierhood: Ayooba Baloch, Farooq Rashid, Shaheed Dar. Three fine young trackers – but as for their dog . . . not all the pooches were bitches.

The prone body of **Saleem** *on the stage now wakes up and joins the 'frozen' scene – and as he joins, the whole plane comes to life.*

Shaheed Hey, Ayooba! Looks like the Indians'll side with the Bengalis!

Ayooba Just let us at 'em, man! Those rice-eater Bonglas! Vegetables always lose to meat. Rice gets mashed. Ka-dang! Ka-pow!

Shaheed *and* **Farooq** *look less sanguine.*

Farooq (*troubled*) But those Sikh troops, yaar. In the heat all that hair pricks like anything, drives them mad, they fight like crazy guys!

Shaheed Sometimes in my dreams I can see my death, you know? It hangs in the air behind me. Looks like a pomegranate. But bright, shining.

Ayooba (*contemptuous*) Quit that defeatist talk, Shaheed, man. Those Bonglas won't beat beefy types like us.

CUTIA Soldier (*referring to* **Saleem**) Ohé, Ayooba! What's that you got there instead of a dog? What kinda mutt is that?

Ayooba This? This old hound dog here is a better sniffer than anything on four legs, that's what! Picked his way through a goddam minefield – he could smell the mines!

Farooq Yah! See that nose on him? He can follow any trail on earth, yaar. Across rocks! Through water!

Shaheed And watch your mouth, okay? He's well connected, too.

Ayooba (*warning him*) Shaheed . . .

Shaheed General Zulfikar's own family, yaar. Why else you think the army took him under its wing?

Brigadier Najmuddin (*pricks up his ears*) Who said that? I'll have no insubordinate talk on this mission!

Ayooba No, nothing, sir. He didn't mean anything. (*to* **Shaheed**) Shut your mouth, why can't you?

Farooq (*to* **CUTIA Soldier**)   He can't remember anything, you know? Not even his name. Can't even talk.

Shaheed (*grumpy at being rebuked*)   Or won't talk.

CUTIA Soldier (*referring to silver spittoon*)   What's your man-dog doing with pukka goods like this?

Saleem *bares his teeth, snarls, hugs the spittoon to his chest.*

Ayooba   Better look out, yaar. You don't want to lose your hand.

CUTIA Soldier   Freak.

Najmuddin *pulls down a map like a roller blind* (*and speaks on a tannoy over the noise of the plane*).

Najmuddin   Pay attention now. No interruptions.

Saleem *barks –* **Najmuddin** *glares.*

Najmuddin   Site of de-planing? Dhaka airport. And your duties are? Pursuit-and-capture. Unusual features? Work in small units – high degree of discipline required.

Saleem *begins to hum 'Do not ask of me, my love'.*

Najmuddin   Silence! Purpose of mission? Rooting out of undesirables. Nature of such elements? Leftists, intellectuals, professors, poets. Number-one target: Sheikh Mujib. Known hideout: Dhaka University. Search without flagging; arrest without remorse. Shoot-while-resisting-arrest. Nose out the enemies of national unity!

Dhaka University. **Professors** *being assaulted and manhandled into a line: manacled, bruised, bleeding.* **Firing Squad** *shoots. The* **Professors** *fall to the ground.*

Farooq   Ayooba, man. It's not true, all of this. It can't be happening.

Shaheed   It isn't happening.

Ayooba To hell with that. You hear me? Shape up, both of you. We've got a job to do.

Saleem *watches, neutral. Then leads them to a door, which they smash down.*

Ayooba Sheikh Mujib! We got the bastard!

Mujib Good evening, gentlemen. You must be well satisfied with your day's work.

Mujib *is bundled by* **Ayooba**, **Shaheed** *and* **Farooq** *to waiting* **CUTIA** Soldiers *and taken away.*

Ayooba (*helpless*) What now?

Saleem *takes off at high speed.*

Shaheed Hey!

Farooq Ohé, yaar! . . . Where's he off to?

Ayooba Don't argue. Just follow that nose. (*to* **Saleem**) Hey! You're on the trail? You're after somebody? You're sure?

Farooq You know him, man. If he's smelt somebody, somebody's there.

Film: throughout this sequence we see an Apocalypse Now-*type jungle backdrop on the screen.*

Jungle swamps. A boat. Monsoon.

Shaheed This is scary, yaar. This is stupid. Could be guerrilla territory. We're sitting ducks.

But **Saleem** *has unfastened the boat – they all board.*

Ayooba Oh, shit.

Dusk. The small boat borne south by the mighty Ganges. The three frightened soldiers crouched in it with **Saleem**.

A **Woman's voice** *sings 'Amar Sonar Bangla' ('Our Golden Bengal') by Tagore in Bengali.*

They float past rice paddies, a village in the middle-distance.

A **Woman's voice** *continues to sing 'Amar Sonar Bangla' in Bengali.*

The boat is swept by river towards the Sundarbans jungle.

Shaheed   We're lost. We're finished. This is where I'll die. Not even in battle.

Farooq (*to* **Saleem**)   Why did we listen to you? You didn't know anything. (*Pause.*) I know why I listened. I was scared. I wanted to run.

The jungle swallows them up.

A labyrinth of salt-water channels beneath trees arching overhead like cathedrals. They are hopelessly lost.

Ayooba   That way, that way!

Shaheed   No, don't be stupid! Down there!

Farooq   I can't see. I don't know. I can't see.

Ayooba *begins to hit* **Saleem.**

Ayooba   You bastard. You didn't know anything. You weren't following anything. You ran away like a coward. And we all followed you, and now we're lost and we're going to die and it's all – your – fault.

The boat runs aground.

A phantasmagoria of a forest. It rains, hard.

Shaheed   The forest. It's growing. It's growing, isn't it?

Ayooba   Shut up.

Farooq   Aagh! Look at our legs!

Their legs are covered in leeches.

Women's *laughter –* **Women** *silhouetted in the trees, above, swinging from tree to tree.*

96

Saleem *follows the* **Women** *into a clearing – a monumental Hindu temple, covered in erotic friezes. A large statue of a black goddess with protruding tongue, multi-limbed, cross-eyed. Remnants of gold paint on her teeth: Kali – who turns into four beautiful young* **Women,** *apparently naked, their eight arms and legs intertwining so that they again resemble the multi-limbed goddess Kali.*

A strange, high-pitched, whining sound in the air.

The **Women** *kiss the soldiers, caress them.*

Ayooba   What the hell . . .?

One of the **Women** *stops his mouth with a kiss. The* **Women** *lie down with the men and make love. The whining noise gets louder.*

Shaheed, Farooq, Ayooba *and* **Saleem** *emerge from the temple.*

Farooq   That didn't happen. It couldn't have.

Shaheed (*appealing to* **Ayooba**)   Did it?

Ayooba *shakes his head – then grins.*

Ayooba   But if it was a dream, it sure was a good one.

Temple. Night. The **Women** *make love to the men. The whining.*

Temple. Day. The men look dazed.

Ayooba   How long have we been here?

Silence.

When did anybody eat anything?

Silence.

This isn't right. We've got to get out.

The **Women** *appear, beckoning the men to make love again.*

Shaheed   No, yaar, are you crazy? These fabulous girls.

Farooq   Who wants to go back to the war, man? We should just wait it out right here.

The whining noise increases. They go towards the **Women** *– who then metamorphose into four charred skeletons.*

Let's scram from here, man. Let's get out now.

Lightning. Thunder. A huge storm has arrived from nowhere.

The men flee the forest of illusions – glimpses of **Women** *in the trees, laughing like monkeys.*

Saleem *takes the lead – running towards the light at the edge of the jungle. They take cover inside a ruined hut.*

Farooq   They'll call us deserters. We'll be court-martialled when we get back.

Shaheed   If we get back.

Ayooba (*to* **Saleem,** *losing his temper*)   If it wasn't for you – yes, you, you dumb freak – I should break your bloody nose!

He advances on **Saleem.** *The whining sound – a bullet. A red stain appears between* **Ayooba's** *eyes. He falls forwards into* **Saleem's** *arms, dead.*

Shaheed   Hindus!

Farooq   O God O God O . . . !

They flatten themselves on the floor – but there is no second shot.

Deshmukh *comes hurrying towards them, grinning ingratiatingly.*

Deshmukh   Plenty shooting! *Thaii! Thaii!* Ho sirs! India has attacked, my sirs! India has come to liberate us. Plenty shooting! India is victor. Ho yes.

They react with disbelief.

Farooq   We lost?

Deshmukh   They had such fighters, my sirs! I have seen with my own eyes one mighty soldier hero! Breaking necks *khrikk-khrikk* between his knees. His knees, Ho God.

Farooq, Shaheed *and* **Saleem** *wander across the corpse-strewn battlefield, pursued by* **Deshmukh**.

Deshmukh   You want watch? Leather belt? Pistol?

He spots **Saleem***'s spittoon, wrapped in rags and slung over his shoulder.*

Ho sir! Is silver? Precious stones? I give you radio, camera. Okay? Damn good deal. Trade must go on! My sirs, life must go on! Ho yes!

The whining. Another bullet . . . **Farooq** *falls to his knees, topples forward, forehead hits the ground where he stays, as if praying, dead.*

Shaheed   Farooq! Farooq, man! No, not you, yaar. It was supposed to be me!

Suddenly, there is a pyramid-like heap of soldier corpses. One corpse – **Hairoil** *– aims his rifle at* **Shaheed** *(he just shot* **Farooq***) but* **Shaheed** *takes the gun and smashes it against him.* **Hairoil** *falls back on the pile – next to the corpse of* **Sonny Ibrahim** *– whose eyes suddenly open.*

Sonny (*to* **Saleem**)   Hullo, man. What the hell are you here for?

Saleem *just stares.*

Sonny   It's Sonny, yaar. Here's **Hairoil** –

Hairoil   Hiya!

Sonny   Remember me? Remember us? Remember?

And just as suddenly, they're all corpses again.

Shaheed *goes to shoot them all, but his gun jams. The corpses all laugh at him.* **Shaheed** *looks up – a hand-grenade* *has been thrown which falls towards him in slow motion. It does indeed look like a pomegranate. It explodes.*

The pile of corpses disintegrates and the explosion erupts into music, the Bangladeshi flag (with its red sun at its centre) and footage. Film of liberation.

Newsreel Announcer A triumph for India's brave liberators, and a triumph for the people of East Pakistan! At last, Dhaka is the free capital of a free country – Bangladesh!

Film (continuous): colour and celebration.

A scene of Indian **Top Brass** *accepting* **Zulfikar***'s surrender – he unsheathes his sword and offers it hilt first.*

Indian Commander Good. That's that. Drink?

Zulfikar Damn decent of you. Don't mind if I do.

Indian Commander (*to one of the* **Top Brass**) Major Shiva? Won't you join us?

Shiva *comes to attention and joins them.*

Indian Commander (*introducing* **Shiva**) Our most decorated hero. One hell of a scrapper.

Zulfikar (*grumpy*) Good show.

Indian victory parade: **Indian Troops** *and* **Army Bands** *followed by* **Magicians***: sorcerers and conjurers and human-pyramid acrobats, contortionists and jugglers, card-tricksters – all from the Delhi Magicians' Ghetto. Music blares: 'Our Golden Bengal' the new nation's anthem.*

Saleem *is bustled through this crowd past the* **Magicians** *with their banner: INDIA'S FAMOUS MAGICIANS! WORLD'S TOP STUNTS! A tall man wreathed in snakes stands beneath a banner proclaiming PICTURE SINGH: THE MOST CHARMING MAN IN THE WORLD – and there is a beautiful woman,* **Parvati-the-Witch** *with her wicker basket (the laundry-basket washing-chest from earlier).*

Parvati   Come on! You want to vanish? Poof, like so? Who is brave enough?

Saleem *is drawn towards her.*

Saleem   Parvati. Parvati-the-witch. (*now realising, now shouting*) Parvati! Parvati-the-witch!

Parvati   Who is it? Who's calling my name?

Saleem *pushes forward and appears before an astonished* **Parvati. Picture Singh** *approaches.*

Picture Singh   Okay, captain – no trouble, now!

Saleem   Parvati. Don't you know me?

Parvati (*shocked*)   Saleem! Is it really you, Saleem?

Saleem (*remembers*)   That was it. 'Saleem'. That's who I was. Saleem Sinai. Snotnose. Bal-die. Sniffer. Map-face. Piece-of-the-Moon. Midnight's Child.

Parvati   It really is you. Arré, too much excitement. For so many years I only dreamed you. And now here you are with a face as glum as a fish.

Zulfikar, *still drinking with the* **Top Brass,** *is shot by an* **Assassin** (*a sniper*). **Zulfikar** *lies dead.*

Pandemonium.

Parvati   Now! Now, Saleem, double quick! In you go! We must get out of here.

She opens the lid of her basket and **Saleem** *dives in head first. She covers him with a sheet and shuts the lid.*

Parvati (*while they're doing this*)   Hey, Saleem. You and me. Midnight's Children. That's something, right? Now that I've found you, I won't let you go.

She whispers magic words.

The **Indian Commander** *suddenly arrives.*

Indian Commander (*of the basket*)   What's in here?

Parvati   Nothing, sir.

The **Indian Commander** *picks up the basket by just one handle – it's evidently very light.*

Picture Singh   Nothing to see, sir.

The basket is empty, except for the sheet, which topples out.

Parvati   You see, sir. Nothing to see.

Padma   Vanished? How vanished, what vanished? Vanished, just like that? Poof, like so?

Region of the Dead. A thick, white, eddying mist. **Saleem** *sitting up in* **Parvati**'s *basket.*

Saleem   Hey! Hello! Is anyone there?

Film: on the screen, **Dead Amina** *appears.*

Dead Amina (*on screen*)   Saleem! How did you get here?

Saleem   I don't know . . . I climbed into Parvati's basket . . .

Dead Amina (*on screen*)   Go back. It isn't your time.

Film: other spectral figures appear – **Aadam Aziz, Reverend Mother, Ahmed, Pia, Vanita, Mian Abdullah, Rani of Cooch Naheen, Lila Sabarmati, Shaheed, Farooq, Zulfikar** *with a fresh bullet hole between his eyebrows. And* **Wee Willie Winkie** *singing 'How much is that doggy in the window'. Then* **Joe.**

Dead Joe (*on screen*)   Poor against rich. That's who we grab our independence from. That's the real revolution.

And other figures emerge on screen.

Dead Hanif (*on screen – greeting* **Saleem**)   Hullo, big fellow! Mister wrestler! Don't look so down!

Dead Sonny (*on screen*)   Hey, man. You made it. No more wars, yaar!

Dead Ayooba (*on screen – miming sex*) Those houris, eh! That was some night patrol!

Dead Emerald (*on screen – with necklace*) Such a helpful boy. Just fasten this, darling.

Saleem This is my place. With all of you. This is where I belong. (*to* **Dead Amina**) Why should I go back?

And then **Dead Jamila** *appears – on stage.*

Jamila! At last!

Dead Jamila This is not the end, Saleem. Not for you. You must go back.

She kisses him on the lips. He closes his eyes . . . and she pushes him, violently – and he tumbles into the Magicians' Ghetto in Old Delhi.

The shadow of a mosque.

Parvati Are you all right?

Saleem I think so . . .

Parvati It was dangerous. Nobody should stay invisible for so long. But how else to bring you home?

Saleem (*remembering*) I was home . . .

Picture Singh Welcome, captain. Welcome to Delhi. I am Picture Singh. They call me the Most Charming Man in the World. Twenty years ago, my picture was all over India. What do you say, captain? A fine likeness, is it not?

He produces a twenty-year-old life-size cardboard photo of himself in which he's holding a camera and covered in snakes – and there's the advertising slogan: 'Charm Your Friends With Eastman-Kodak'.

But let me warn you about this bunch of bastards. Communists! The lot of them.

The **Magicians** *cheer.*

That's right: reds! Insurrectionists, public menaces, the scum of the earth!

The **Magicians** *erupt into spontaneous fire-breathing, acrobatic tumbling, pratfalls, etc.*

I have warned them about their Trotskys, their Ho Chi Minnies.

The **Magicians** *mock 'boo'.*

There are no rabbits in those guys' hats, I tell them. But seems like even magicians can fall for politicos' cheap tricks.

Saleem   And Parvati?

Picture Singh   Parvati? No, no. Parvati is a sensible girl. But an orphan, captain. What to do? She is your good friend. Any ideas?

Whistles and catcalls from the **Magicians** *–* **Parvati** *blushes and, picking up her basket, goes to her humble shack.* **Saleem** *follows.*

Parvati   At last I have someone who knows my magic is real. Did you ever see a magician who believed in magic? They think everything's a trick.

Saleem   Why don't you tell them?

Parvati (*laughing*)   Ha! They'd stone me. They don't want any real witches around here.

Saleem   Not even Picture Singh?

Parvati   Not even Picture Singh.

Saleem   But now there's me.

Parvati   Yes. Now there's you.

They begin to make love. **Jamila** *appears on the screen, seducing* **Saleem**, *who lies back and dreamily watches* **Jamila** *as* **Parvati** *makes love on top.*

Saleem   I couldn't. I just couldn't make love to her. I couldn't get Jamila out of my head. So I did a terrible thing.

I told a lie . . . which, soon enough, became the truth.

*The Magicians' Ghetto. The **Magicians** practise their tricks, their performances, their antics. **Saleem** and **Picture Singh** stroll among them.*

Picture Singh   Listen, captain, you like the girl, eh? Planning to be married soon?

Saleem (*panicking*)   Pictureji, I can't.

Picture Singh *stops in his tracks.*

Saleem   No point my marrying anyone. I . . . I can't have children.

Picture Singh (*dismayed*)   You're telling the truth, captain? To lie about your manhood is bad, bad luck. Anything could happen, captain.

Saleem (*angry, as he compounds the lie*)   I tell you, it's true; and that's that!

Picture Singh   Then, captain, God knows what to do with that poor girl.

Saleem   How could I tell her that her face changed into someone else's every night? How to explain I'd been making love to a ghost?

Parvati's *shack.* **Parvati** and **Saleem**.

Parvati   But why won't you make love to me any more? Haven't we been happy?

Silence.

You're too grand for me, is that it? With your grand family and all? Ha! They left you in the gutter – like a dog.

Silence.

Midnight's Children. Big deal.

Pause.

105

Anyway, big shot. You're not the only one I know.

Saleem What do you mean?

Parvati *rummages for a locket in which is a lock of dark hair.*

Parvati I saw him one day in Connaught Place. The biggest hero of that whole war, when you just hid in the jungle. He's a big officer now. Got promotion. He let me cut this right from his head.

Saleem Who?

Parvati Major Shiva. Your old buddy. You know: the one who hates your guts. The one with the superpower knees. Maybe you should just go, and I'll send for him. You think he won't come? Don't be so sure. (*stroking the lock of hair*) Remember me? I'm the witch.

Saleem *walks out.*

Film.

Newsreel Announcer Accusations of corruption dog Mrs Indira Gandhi and her beloved Sanjay! Mrs Gandhi charged with electoral malpractice! Indira is reeling, pundits say!

Parvati (*conjuring*) Come-to-me! Abracadabra-abracadabra-abracadabra-come-to-me!

And **Shiva** *roars into the Magicians' Ghetto.*

Shiva What the hell am I doing here? Who the hell are you?

Parvati Major Shiva. Welcome. I am Parvati.

Shiva I don't give a fuck who you are. I'm leaving.

But as he heads off, he stops.

Parvati You're not leaving.

He turns back to her, caught in her spell.

Come here.

He lies beside her, unbuttoning his uniform.

You and me, yaar. Midnight's Children, remember? That's something. That's really something.

And they kiss and make love.

Parvati (*kneeling at* **Shiva***'s feet*)   I am going to have your child.

Shiva   I don't give a fuck about your child. I don't give a fuck about you. Get away from me. . . How are you doing this? . . . Let me go! . . . I've got to get away from you.

He is straining against some invisible force, but can't leave.

Parvati (*suddenly tired of him*)   You can go.

He goes.

And here comes **Parvati** *from her hut – now heavily pregnant.*

Saleem   I saw Parvati carrying the child of my arch enemy – and trapped in the web of interweaving genealogies, I chose parenthood for myself. Once again a child was to be born to a father who was not his father. I married Parvati-the-witch.

Wedding night, in the hut, after the celebration. The pregnant **Parvati** *is garlanded and laughing for joy.* **Saleem** *is turbaned and garlanded and flower petals are strewn everywhere.*

Picture Singh   Hey, captain! Need any pointers? Any tips?

Contortionist (*twisting herself up*)   Ohé, Parvati! Want to learn some positions?

Parvati (*laughing*)   Go away! All of you! Vanish!

Picture Singh   At once, madam! Poof! Like so!

And they do, leaving **Saleem** *and* **Parvati** *alone in the shack. They kiss tenderly.*

Saleem (*realising something*) Your face. It's still your face.

Parvati (*puzzled*) What about my face? Something wrong?

Saleem No. That's just it. There's nothing wrong. There's nothing wrong at all.

He kisses her with great love. But:

Parvati What's the matter?

Saleem Have you put a clock in here?

Parvati Of course not, stupid. From where would a clock suddenly appear?

Tick, tock. Tick, tock!

Newsreel Announcer At two p.m. this afternoon, June the twelfth 1975, Prime Minister Indira Gandhi was found guilty of electoral malpractice.

Parvati *clutches herself with a cry – then clutches* **Saleem**.

Parvati It's started!

Tick, tock.

Newsreel Announcer At precisely two p.m. today, Parvati-the-witch went into labour.

Film: newsreel: Indira Gandhi, looking glum at her New Delhi residence.

Mrs Gandhi has refused to resign!

Parvati *shrieks –* **Older Women** *in attendance.*

Newsreel Announcer Meanwhile, the cervix of Parvati-the-witch obstinately refuses to dilate!

Film: newsreel: demonstrators outside the Prime Minister's house.

Noisy protestors fill the streets!

Parvati *screams.*

Newsreel Announcer   Parvati, too, makes noisy protests!

Parvati   Aaah! Aaaah! Aaaaah!

Film: newsreel: press conference with leaders of Opposition and banners saying REMOVE INDIRA, etc.

Newsreel Announcer   The Opposition tries hard to push Indira from power.

Parvati, *exhausted, straining hard.*

Newsreel Announcer   Parvati also tries hard to push!

Parvati   Uhhh . . . Uhhh . . . Uhhh . . .

Film: newsreel: national emergency, Central Reserve Police vehicles screech down streets, sirens blaring, lights flashing.

Newsreel Announcer   Finally, at midnight on the twenty-sixth of June, the Emergency is born! – and, at the same moment, Parvati's child also emerges! A ten-chip whopper!

Saleem   Aadam Sinai was born in Old Delhi . . . once upon a time. No, that won't do, it's important to be more . . . on the stroke of midnight as a matter of fact. Clock-hands joined palms. He was the child of a father who was not his father; but also the child of a time which damaged reality so badly that nobody ever managed to put it together again.

Pickle factory.

Padma   Dark or fair? Hair or no hair? How many pounds? Was it okay?

Saleem   The new Emergency – no, it wasn't really okay.

Padma   The *baby*, bhai. Who did it look like? Tell me something about it, na. Must've been beautiful.

Saleem   Ugly, Padma. Dark and ugly. It had fully suspended civil rights. It came with total censorship. So ugly, it even stopped the clocks. And there began a two-year-long, unbroken midnight.

Padma Enough, baba. Enough about that. Just tell me about your child.

Saleem You'll see. You've seen.

Padma Arré . . .

Saleem He was a sweet boy, Padma. A boy with ears.

Padma Ears?

Saleem *Big* ears. He was the true great-grandson of his great-grandfather, but elephantiasis attacked him in the ears instead of the nose – because he was also the true son of Shiva-and-Parvati, he was the elephant-headed Ganesh . . .

Magicians' Ghetto. The rumble of an advancing line of bulldozers. Floodlights.

Shiva (*through loudhailer*) Civic beautification programme . . . authorised operation of Sanjay Youth Central Committee . . . this slum is a public eyesore, it can no longer be tolerated . . .

Figures descend – beds, surgical equipment, hastily erected.

Saleem Vasectomy! Sterilisation! Look out! Save yourselves!

Bulldozers destroy the ghetto. Men and women dragged to beds.

Saleem (*screaming*) Parvati! Baby Aadam! No!!!

He's knocked forward by **Shiva**.

Shiva (*knees pinning* **Saleem** *to the ground*) So, little rich boy: we meet again. I've been looking for you.

Saleem Shiva . . . save them . . . Parvati . . . Baby Aadam . . .

Shiva (*into radio*) Project MCC. Objective A achieved.

Saleem *is shackled and led away.*

Padma Where did they take you?

Film: images of the holy city of Benares, seen from the water.

Saleem To a holy city, Padma, for unholy deeds. To the city of light. In that dark time. Kashi, Padma. Varanasi. They took me to Benares.

He is shown into an interrogation room – chair – light – **Shiva** *presides, with* **Thin Man, Fat Man** *in attendance.*

Saleem What is this? Some madhouse?

Shiva Old maharaja palace, requisitioned by us.

Saleem Who's 'us'?

Shiva Shut your face. This is Project MCC . . . Midnight's Children Conference. 'Indiraji is determined to eradicate the problem.' That's what this is all about. Many things happen in an Emergency. Already the trains are running on time. Black-money hoarders have been scared into paying their taxes. And subversives of all sorts are being neutralised. How many? (*he shrugs*) Thirty thousand. A quarter of a million. A small percentage of the population of India. Your gang of freaks will also be smashed. With your help.

Saleem Traitor. You think I'm going to help you?

Thin Man Oh, yes. Names, addresses.

Fat Man Physical descriptions, nature of . . . peculiar capabilities. Thanking you in advance.

Saleem Go to hell.

Fat Man *and* **Thin Man** *smile. Lights off.* **Saleem** *screams.*

Lights on. **Saleem** *whimpers.*

Fat Man His conscience is still troubling him.

Thin Man We'll wait until his conscience clears.

Fat Man (*to* **Saleem**) You're doing very well.

Lights off. **Saleem** *screams.*

Lights on.

Thin Man   There! I told you you could do it.

Fat Man   That wasn't so bad, was it? Not so bad at all.

Saleem *weeps, uncontrollably. Lights out.*

Lights on. **Saleem**'s *face is beaten, bleeding, swollen.*

Saleem   Shiva . . .

Thin Man   What did he say?

Fat Man   Hard to tell.

Saleem   He's one, too.

Thin Man   One two what?

Saleem   He's really me. I'm really him.

Fat Man   He doesn't know what he's saying.

Saleem   Born together. Same place, same time. Then . . . a mistake.

Shiva *is now interested – his face close to* **Saleem**'s.

Shiva   What's this nonsense? What mistake?

Saleem   The babies. You're really me. I'm really you.

Thin Man   Are you following this, Major?

Fat Man   It's some sort of fixation.

Shiva (*enraged as it dawns on him*)   Bastard. Haramzada.

Saleem   Swapped, see? Sssss . . . whapped. (*giggles*) I stole your life.

Shiva   Shut up! Madman!

Saleem   That's how I know your mother was a whore.

Shiva *takes out his pistol and puts it against* **Saleem**'s *forehead, right between the eyes – but then pistol-whips him.* **Saleem** *falls to the floor.*

Saleem The truest, deepest motive behind the declaration of a State of Emergency was the smashing and the pulverising of Midnight's Children. I betrayed the children of midnight – they poured, blubbering, from my lips: names addresses physical descriptions. Children, children, I'm sorry.

Later: the door opens. A **Woman** *enters with* **Shiva**. *She is voluptuous, gorgeous, in a green-and-black expensive silk sari.*

Shiva (*to* **Saleem**) You! Stand to attention.

Saleem *struggles to do so, but falls back to the floor.* **Shiva** *goes to strike him with his pistol.*

Sari Woman No, no. We owe this gentleman a great deal. He has told us so much. Certainly we owe him an explanation. (*to* **Saleem**) Think of me as one of the great lady's many right hands. For she is, one may say, multi-limbed, like a goddess.

Saleem (*faintly*) A goddess.

Sari Woman (*breezily*) Oh, yes. For the masses, our Lady is the manifestation of Devi. Let me tell you in confidence that it has taken us ages to create this impression.

Saleem Then why us? What are we to you?

She leans close to him and smiles a sweet, terrible smile. Then she rises, turns to go.

Sari Woman I regret to inform you that we will be obliged to operate.

Saleem What are you talking about? What operation?

Sari Woman (*leaving*) I like to call it . . . sperectomy.

She exits with **Shiva**.

Saleem What about him???

An iron anaesthesia mask descends over **Saleem's** *face.*

. . . Two, three . . . four hundred million . . . five hundred, six . . . mmff . . .

(fast, monotone) The walls are green the sky is black the Widow is green her teeth are black her tongue is green her fingernails are long and sharp and black.

The Widow's arm comes snaking down the snake is green her heart is black. And one by one the children scream and little balls and splashing stains of black. And in a corner she and I . . . in a corner . . . in a corner . . .

Good doctors, eh, children? The best. Testicles removed, wombs snatched away. Testectomy, hysterectomy. And they cut the midnight magic away, too, how did they do that, but they did. No more flying, eh, children, no more miracles of fishes or words that can kill. No more alchemy. The children of midnight were denied the possibility of reproducing themselves. They were sterilised. Sperectomy, she said, eh? Sper – ect – omy. The cutting out of hope. We were the hope of freedom. And, like all hope, born to be crushed.

Saleem *caught in a shaft of light.*

Newsreel Announcer   Three years later. March 1977. In a stunning upset, Shrimati Indira Gandhi has been unceremoniously flung out of office!

Saleem – *filthy, bewildered, emerges outside the prison.*

Newsreel Announcer   Many of Mrs Gandhi's so-called 'right hands' have been taken into custody. Others have absconded and are presently on the run!

Dawn: sunrise.

Outside the prison, **Picture Singh,** *holding the hand of* **Little Aadam** – *who is now three years old – is waiting for* **Saleem.** *Who comes towards him, filthy, broken, in a daze.*

Picture Singh   Captain, greetings.

Saleem Picture Singh . . . where's Parvati . . . ?

Picture Singh I'm sorry . . . she did not survive.

Saleem *puts his hands over his face.*

Picture Singh But here is your son.

Saleem *hugs and hugs* **Little Aadam.**

Picture Singh Come on, captain. Let's wash that filthy place out of your hair. Out of your heart.

Saleem *washes, as, on screen,* **Shiva** *drives a motorbike, at crazy, reckless speed, driving as if he wants to die. There is a crash.*

Saleem And what of Shiva? He died. It was an accident. Perhaps.

Later. **Picture Singh** *brings* **Saleem** *a simple thali of rice and dhal. From a Braganza Pickles jar he scoops out some green chutney for* **Saleem.** **Little Aadam** *is on* **Saleem'***s lap. He lifts him up and hands him to* **Picture Singh** *so that he can eat.*

Saleem Thank you for looking after him.

Picture Singh He doesn't talk, captain. Listens to everything but doesn't let out one word. Maybe he's the careful type.

Pause.

So what now for you, captain?

Saleem I don't know. I feel used up.

Picture Singh You have a son now, captain. Responsibilities. A fine child, captain. A child of dignity. You hardly notice his ears.

Saleem *tastes the chutney, and recognises the taste. Until this moment he has seemed dull, spent, ever since he emerged from prison. Now animation, even excitement returns.*

Saleem This chutney . . . what is it? Where's it from?

Picture Singh   Braganza Pickles, captain. Best in Bombay. Everyone knows.

Saleem (*leaps to his feet*)   Pictureji, I have to go. I have to.

Picture Singh (*hugging* **Little Aadam**)   Then go.

Saleem   But how can I leave you?

Picture Singh   Don't be a fool, captain. You have something you must do. It is your quest. What do I want with you? You think Little Aadam needs me as his ayah? I tell you, captain, there is nothing to do but to do it. Go. Quickly. Go.

And **Saleem** *takes* **Little Aadam**, *leaving behind* **Picture Singh**, *and pursues the pickle factory. Film: all the past, places, people.*

A winking, saffron-and-green neon goddess over the factory gate of Braganza Pickles (Private) Ltd. **Saleem** *enters the gates.*

Saleem   And when I finally arrived, who answered the door? Who at the end of my road, gave me the once-over, and asked me if I was crazy in the head?

Padma   You, mister: what you want? – Me! Of course, who else? Me me me! –

Saleem   Good morning, Begum.

Padma   O you – always so polite an all!

Saleem   I'm sorry to disturb you so early. Is Mrs Braganza here? This chutney; may I speak to the manager?

Padma   Not possible. Mrs Braganza asleep. Come back later. Please go away just now.

Saleem   No, you don't understand . . .

There is a shriek from **Mrs Braganza**'s *office – we see her face sticking out, still in silhouette.*

Mrs Braganza   Arré baap! Baapu-ré . . . ! Saleem???

Saleem   Mrs Braganza?

Mrs Braganza   O my God! O my God! O Jesus! Sweet Jesus! Saleem! Oh, baba, my son, my one true son, look who's come here, look how thin you got, come, come let me kiss you, let me give you cake!

Now, at last, we see who she is as she smothers **Saleem** *in kisses.*

Saleem   Mrs Braganza? Mary Pereira? Mary?

Mary (*of* **Little Aadam**)   Your son?

Saleem   It's a long story.

Padma   Begin at the beginning.

Saleem   Well . . .

Little Aadam *makes a sound.*

Mary   Arré, o my God, listen, baba, the boy is saying something.

Little Aadam   Abba . . .

Saleem   Abba. Father. He's calling me father.

Little Aadam   Abbaracadabra!

Saleem *gives* **Mary Little Aadam** – *she holds the child as she used to hold* **Saleem**. *A beautiful tableau.*

The song of **Mary Pereira**.
   Anything you want to be you can be;
   You can be just what-all you want . . .

And now **Saleem** *is sitting at the desk closing the thirtieth red exercise book (only one remains).*

Saleem   The End.

Padma   My God. And that's your life? And it's all true?

Saleem   Mostly.

Padma *indicates the remaining, unused exercise book.*

Padma   What's that for?

Saleem (*shrugs*)   I don't know. After the end. The future.

Padma (*ruffling the pages*)   Maybe our future?

Saleem   Maybe.

Padma (*overjoyed, kissing him*)   O, mister. O, mister. I'll tell madam.

She goes out. **Saleem** *looks through the exercise books.*

Saleem   All the eggs which gave birth to the population of India could be fitted into a standard-size pickle jar. All the spermatozoa could be lifted on a single spoon. Every pickle jar contains, therefore, an amazing possibility: the chutnification of history. I, however, have pickled stories: memories and histories, vegetables and fruit. These (*the books*) are the pickles of history. And they are, despite everything, acts of love.

Film: on screen, we fast-forward through Indian history from 1978 to the present day and end at a vast crowd celebrating Independence Day in modern-day India, now . . .

The future? How to tell Padma . . . there's no future. Not for me. Tick, tock. It's Independence Day again and the many-headed multitude will be in the streets pushing shoving crushing, and the cracks, my cracks, will widen . . . I can hear and feel the rip tear crunch.

Padma *returns with a birthday cake.*

Padma   Happy birthday, mister! Happy birthday!

Conch-shell blasts. The sea of humanity dwarfs **Saleem.**

Saleem   Yes, they will trample me underfoot, the numbers marching one two three, four hundred million, five hundred, six . . .

Film: . . . and as at the beginning of the play, the film bleeds into other aspects of modern India, but this time they are darker, more distressing, more violent sides of the nation . . .

. . . just as they will trample my son who is not my son, and his who will not be his, until the thousand and first generation.

Because it is the privilege and the curse of midnight's children to be both masters and victims of their times, to forsake privacy and be sucked into the annihilating whirlpool of the multitudes, and to be unable to live or die in peace.

Introducing the RSC

The Royal Shakespeare Company is one of the world's best-known theatre ensembles. The Company is widely regarded as one of the most important interpreters of Shakespeare and other dramatists. Today the RSC is at the leading edge of classical theatre, with an international reputation for artistic excellence, accessibility and high-quality live performance.

Our mission at the Royal Shakespeare Company is to create outstanding theatre relevant to our times through the work of Shakespeare, other Renaissance dramatists, international and contemporary writers. Every year the Company plays to a million theatregoers at 2,000 performances, including over 50 weeks of UK and international touring.

We want to give as many people as possible, from all walks of life, a richer and fuller understanding and enjoyment of language and theatre. Through education and outreach programmes we continually strive to engage people with the experience of live performance.

The RSC's touchstone is the work of William Shakespeare. We are committed to presenting the widest range of Shakespeare's plays and demonstrating through performance the international and enduring appeal of his plays. We also want to inspire contemporary writers with the ambition of the Renaissance stage, presenting new plays alongside classical theatre.

The Company's roots in Stratford-upon-Avon stretch back to the nineteenth century. However, since the 1960s, the RSC's work in Stratford has been complemented by a regular presence in London. But Stratford and London are only part of the story. Over 25 years of residency in the city of Newcastle upon Tyne have forged a profound link between RSC artists and audiences in the north-east of England. Many of our productions also visit major regional theatres around Britain. And our annual regional tour sets up its own travelling auditorium in community centres, sports halls and schools in towns throughout the UK without access to professional theatre.

While the UK is the home of the Company, our audiences are global. The company regularly plays to enthusiastic theatregoers in other parts of Europe, across the United States, the Americas, Asia and Australasia. The RSC is proud of its relationships with partnering organisations in other countries, particularly in America.

Despite continual change, the RSC today is still at heart an ensemble Company. The continuation of this great tradition informs the work of all members of the Company. Directors, actors, dramatists and theatre practitioners all collaborate in the creation of the RSC's distinctive and unmistakable approach to theatre.

THE ROYAL SHAKESPEARE
COMPANY

Patron	Her Majesty the Queen
President	His Royal Highness the Prince of Wales
Deputy President	Sir Geoffrey Cass MA CIMgt
Chairman of the Board	Lord Alexander of Weedon QC
Deputy Chairman	Lady Sainsbury of Turville
Vice-Chairmen	Charles Flower, Professor Stanley Wells PhD, DLitt

Direction:
Artistic Director	Adrian Noble
Managing Director	Chris Foy
Executive Producer	Lynda Farran
Advisory Direction	John Barton, David Brierley, Peter Brook, Trevor Nunn
Emeritus Directors	Trevor Nunn, Terry Hands
Associate Directors	Michael Boyd, Gregory Doran

Casting:
Resident Casting Director	John Cannon

Development:
Development Director	Liam Fisher-Jones
Head of Development	Paula Flinders

Dramaturgy:
Dramaturg   Paul Sirett

Education:
Director of Education   Clare Venables
Head of Learning
Programmes   Trevelyan Wright

Finance and Administration:
Director of Finance
and Administration   David Fletcher
Head of Finance   Donna Gribben
Head of
Information Technology   Chris O'Brien
Senior Management
Accountant   Elaine Smith

Human Resources:
Head of Human
Resources   Rachael Whitteridge
Health and Safety Adviser   Gail Miller

Marketing:
Director of Marketing   Kate Horton
Marketing Manager
(Research and Development)   Melanie Bloxham
Marketing Manager
(Campaign)   Chris Hill
Sales Manager   John Pinchbeck
Retail Manager   Justin Tose
Head of Graphics   Andy Williams

Music:
Head of Music &
Associate Artist   Stephen Warbeck
Music Manager   Kate Andrew
Director of Music (London)   Richard Brown
Music Adviser   Michael Tubbs

Company Music Director	John Woolf
Planning Administration:	
Planning Administrator	Carol Malcolmson
Press and Public Affairs:	
Director of Press and Public Affairs	Roger Mortlock
Head of Press	Philippa Harland
Community Liaison Manager	Peter Coombs
Producer:	
Producer	Denise Wood
Technical and Production:	
Technical Director	Geoff Locker
Production Manager	Simon Ash
Head of Construction and Technical Design	Alan Bartlett
Head of Engineering Services	Simon Bowler
Technical Co-ordinator	Steve Carlin
Head of Sound	Jeremy Dunn
Property Workshop Manager	John Evans
Engineering Manager (Stratford)	Peter Fordham CEng
Production Manager	Mark Graham
Production Manager	Peter Griffin
Lighting Supervisor	Michael Gunning
Scenic Workshop Manager	Paul Hadland
Stage Supervisor	Roger Haymes
Head of Lighting	Vince Herbert
Wigs and Make-up Supervisor	Brenda Leedham
Head of Paint Shop	Nigel Loomes
Production Manager	David Parker
Design Co-ordinator	Anthony Rowe

Head of Maintenance
Wardrobe   Barbara Stone

Projects:
Project Administrator   Caro MacKay
Project Administrator   Jeremy Adams

Stratford Re-development:
Project Director   Jonathan Pope

Theatre Operations:
London Manager   Neil Constable
Theatres Manager (Stratford) Richard Rhodes
Stratford Manager   Gary Stewart

Voice:
Head of Voice   Andrew Wade
Senior Voice Coach   Lyn Darnley